Son of 'Curried Eggs'

ALSO BY ROGER WILMUT

The Goon Show Companion
Tony Hancock: 'Artiste'
From Fringe to Flying Circus

COMPILED BY ROGER WILMUT

'No More Curried Eggs For Me'

Son of 'Curried Eggs'

A second helping of classic comedy sketches
compiled by ROGER WILMUT

METHUEN · LONDON

First published in Great Britain in 1984 by
Methuen London Ltd,
11 New Fetter Lane, London EC4P 4EE
Printed in Great Britain

Preface and introductory notes
copyright © 1984 by Roger Wilmut
This selection
copyright © 1984 by Methuen London Ltd

British Library Cataloguing in Publication Data

Son of 'Curried eggs'.
1. English wit and humour
I. Wilmut, Roger
827′.914′08 PN6175

ISBN 0–413–55170–9

Grateful acknowledgement is due to the copyright owners of the individual sketches for permission to reprint them in this volume:

To Graham Chapman and John Cleese for 'At Last the 1948 Show'; to Alan Bennett for 'Take a Pew'; to Peter Cook for 'The Man Who Invented the Wheel'; to Peter Cook and Dudley Moore for 'Disease'; to Frank Muir and Denis Norden for 'A Saga of Sixpence'; to Spike Milligan and the Estate of the Late Larry Stephens for 'The Histories of Pliny the Elder'; to Macmillan, London and Basingstoke, for 'George – Don't Do That' by Joyce Grenfell; to Ray Galton and Alan Simpson for 'Hancock's Car'; to Douglas Adams for 'The Hitch-Hiker's Guide to the Galaxy'; to Jonathan Miller for 'The Heat-Death of the Universe'; to Barry Took for 'Julian and Sandy – Bona Political Party'; to Eric Idle for 'Wife-swopping Party Song'; to Jonathan Lynn and Antony Jay for 'The Moral Dimension'.

CONTENTS

PREFACE

Yes, I know *Son of 'Curried Eggs'* is a damn silly title for a book. The 'Curried Eggs' bit comes from my previous book of comedy scripts, where it was lifted from the Goon Show quoted there. As for 'Son of . . .', well I suppose it was Rudolf Valentino who started that, with *Son of the Sheik*, made in 1926 as a sequel to *The Sheik*. Since then of course we have had *Son of Frankenstein*, *Son of Kong*, *Son of Godzilla* . . . I know it hasn't got anything to do with this book, it's just a way of trying to cover up the fact that I couldn't think of a better title.

Once again, the book contains a collection of favourite comedy scripts; in most cases they are transcribed from the original broadcasts in order to reflect the usual last minute changes made to the text.

My thanks are due to the people who wrote all this material and kindly allowed me to use it; and to the BBC Script Library, Antony Jay and Jonathan Lynn, Tim Smith, and Peter Copeland for provision of research material.

ROGER WILMUT

'AT LAST THE 1948 SHOW'

This show, to which *Monty Python's Flying Circus* was the natural successor, consisted of two series of six episodes broadcast by Independent Television in 1967. John Cleese and Graham Chapman wrote this sketch, which foreshadows the sadistic element in Monty Python, and it was performed by Tim Brooke-Taylor (as the interviewer) and Graham Chapman (as the shepherd) in the show first broadcast on 1 March 1967.

'Sheepdog Trials'

B-TAYLOR: Well good morning from the National Sheepdog Trials at Tinnertern. We've had a fascinating morning here watching these truly intelligent dogs perform complex tasks guided only by the whistles of their masters. Now I have with me Mr. Leigh. Good morning, Mr. Leigh.

CHAPMAN: Baa! I mean, good morning.

B-TAYLOR: Mr. Leigh, I believe you've been a shepherd now for over forty years?

CHAPMAN: Oh, no – no, no, no – I've been a shepherd now for over thirty-five years – sixty-eight years I've been a shepherd now. Man and boy – not in that order, of course.

B-TAYLOR: Well, in your life you must have trained many sheepdogs.

CHAPMAN: Oh, yes.

(Pause.)

B-TAYLOR: How many?

CHAPMAN: Oh, well over two.

B-TAYLOR: Over two? Well, well, well, two . . . well, how do you train the dogs?

CHAPMAN: Oh, that's very simple, we use a little kindness and a lot of cruelty.

B-TAYLOR: Oh – you have to be cruel to the dogs?

CHAPMAN: Oh yes, very cruel, very cruel indeed – I'm surprised it's allowed. Really nasty. Shocking. And sadistic we are with 'em.

B-TAYLOR: And the dogs drive the sheep?

CHAPMAN: The dogs drive the sheep into the pen – it's known as 'filling your pen' – ha-har! – shepherd's joke, shepherd's joke, that! And very funny too!

B-TAYLOR: Yes . . . and how do they drive the sheep?

CHAPMAN: You are a nosy old turnip, aren't you. Well, I tell 'ee, my old dear . . . The dogs bark at the sheep, then they crawls up to them on their bellies, then they nudges them with their noses, then they buries their fangs in 'em.

B-TAYLOR: Oh . . . and then the dogs herd the sheep into

the pens?

CHAPMAN: Ar. Sometimes the sheep drive *them* into the pen, and then the dogs just sit there looking embarrassed, and everyone laughs at 'em, and I laughs at 'em too – I think it's very funny. My wife – she thinks it's funny.

B-TAYLOR: Does she really.

CHAPMAN: Got a great sense of humour, my wife.

B-TAYLOR: I'd like to meet her some time.

CHAPMAN: Ever since her accident.

B-TAYLOR: I'm sorry to hear that. . . . How many sheepdogs have you?

CHAPMAN: 'Tis a secret, I'm not telling you . . . 'tis a most holy secret that cannot and must not be divulged. Two.

B-TAYLOR: Oh, you have two dogs?

CHAPMAN: Shh!

B-TAYLOR *(whispering)*: You have two dogs?

CHAPMAN: Yes.

B-TAYLOR: Where are they now?

CHAPMAN: Oh ar, well one of them's over – now where is he? Ar – over there by that pile of dead sheep. Magnificent brute – treacherous to a fault. Just has this little weakness for mutton.

B-TAYLOR: Do the dogs kill the sheep?

CHAPMAN: Only in fun. Still, that's better than burying them in the ground and pulling their heads off – it's more humane.

B-TAYLOR: Yes – well, perhaps you could get your dogs to give us a demonstration.

CHAPMAN: Oh, you don't need the dogs for that, you just bury the sheep in the ground . . .

B-TAYLOR: No, no – could you get the dogs to drive the sheep into the pen?

CHAPMAN: I've only got old Butcher here at the moment – I don't know where Crippen's gone to. He must be off after the judges – he senses they're his natural enemies.

B-TAYLOR: Well, could you just put Butcher through his paces, then?

CHAPMAN: All right – I'll get him to drive that sheep into that pen over there. Right . . . *(whistles)*

(Frantic baa-ing noises from off-screen.)

B-TAYLOR: Surely, Mr. Leigh, he shouldn't be . . . Mr. Leigh, what *is* he doing? Surely he shouldn't be *eating* that sheep?!

CHAPMAN: You shut your mouth!

B-TAYLOR: Oh, goodness me – how awful! Oh, this is embarrassing!

CHAPMAN *(shouting at the off-screen dog)*: STOP THAT, YOU THIEVIN' CUR, OR I'LL TEAR YOU APART WITH MY BARE HANDS! *(To B-Taylor:)* Ar, look at that – I swear he understands every word I say!

ALAN BENNETT

When *Beyond the Fringe* transferred to the West End of London after its successful run at the 1960 Edinburgh Festival, the top theatrical producer Donald Albery came to see the final run-through. His verdict was along the lines of 'It will be all right except for the fair-haired one'. The fair-haired one was Alan Bennett, who subsequently commented: 'I did understand what he meant'. Had Albery had his way and removed Bennett from the cast, the revue would never have had its resounding success, for Bennett's pin-sharp observation was an essential ingredient of the show. Nowhere was this more apparent than in his sermon, which has the alarming effect of causing every other sermon one ever hears to sound exactly like it.

'Take a Pew'

The eleventh verse of the twenty-seventh chapter of the book of Genesis: 'And he said, My brother Esau is an hairy man, but I am a smooth man.' And he said, my brother Esau is an hairy man, but *I* am a smooth man.

Perhaps I might say the same thing in a different way, by quoting you those words of that grand old English poet W. E. Henley, who said:

'When that one great scorer comes
To mark against your name
It matters not who won, or lost—
But how you played the game.'

But how you played the game. Words very meaningful and significant for us, here, together, tonight. Words we might do very much worse than to consider. And I use this word, 'consider', advisedly, because I'm using it, you see, in its original Greek sense of 'con-sider'. Of putting oneself in the way of thinking about something. I want us, here, together, tonight, to put ourselves in the way of thinking about . . . to put ourselves in the way of thinking about . . . what we *ought* to be putting ourselves in the way of thinking about.

As I was on my way here tonight, I arrived at the station, and by an oversight I happened to go out by the way one is supposed to come in; and as I was going out an employee of the railway company hailed me. 'Hey Jack,' he shouted, 'where do you think you're going?' That at any rate was the gist of what he said. But, you know, I was grateful to him; because, you see, he put me in mind of the kind of question I felt I ought to be asking you here tonight. Where do you think *you're* going?

Very many years ago, when I was about as old as some of you are now, I went mountain climbing in Scotland with a very dear friend of mine. And there was this mountain, you see, and we decided to climb it. And so, very early one morning, we arose and began to climb. All day we climbed. Up and up and up; higher and higher and higher. Until the valley lay very small below us, and the mists of the evening began to come down, and the sun to set. And when we reached the summit we sat down to watch this magnificent sight of the sun going down behind the mountain. And as he watched, my friend very suddenly and violently vomited.

Some of us think Life's a bit like that, don't we? But it isn't. Life, you know, is rather like opening a tin of sardines. We are all of us looking for the key. And I wonder, how many of you here tonight have wasted years of your lives looking behind the kitchen dressers of this life for that key. I know I have. Others think they've found the key, don't they? They roll back the lid of the sardine tin of Life, they reveal the sardines, the riches of Life, therein, and they get them out, they enjoy them. But, you know, there's always a little bit in the corner you can't get out. I wonder – I wonder, is there a little bit in the corner of your life? I know there is in mine.

And so now I draw to a close. I want you, when you go out into the world, in times of trouble, and sorrow, and hopelessness, and despair, amid the hurly-burly of modern life, if ever you're tempted to say, 'Stuff this for a lark'; I want you, at such times, to cast your minds back to the words of my first text to you tonight. 'But my brother Esau is an hairy man, but *I* am a smooth man.'

PETER COOK

Peter Cook's character E. L. Wisty first appeared, though un-named, in *Beyond the Fringe*, in the monologue about the miner who wanted to be a judge. In ITV's 1965 series *On The Braden Beat* Cook did a regular appearance as E. L. Wisty, sitting on a park bench and staring glassy-eyed into the camera. This is a typical example:

'The Man Who Invented the Wheel'

During the last few weeks I've been trying to think of something absolutely original and devastating. I've been trying to lay me hands on some idea that'll revolutionize the world in some way. Something like fire, or the wheel. 'Course, it's no good thinking of those two because they've already been invented, but something along those lines. It's a very good thing to do, you know. I mean, look at the man who thought of fire. He could have made an absolute fortune. As soon as he thought of it he should have patented it, and every time anybody lit a fire they'd have had to pay him a royalty. But being a rather primitive person he didn't think of that.

The same thing happened to the bloke who thought of the wheel. Actually nobody really knows who was the first person to invent the wheel. It's all shrouded in mystery. Apparently, in primeval times, there were these two primitive people, who were both working on inventions in their caves. They were called Drodbar and Gorbly. Two extremely primitive people. Then one day Drodbar came out with a great smile all over his hairy face, and he said, 'Guess what – I've just invented the ban-dan-bladder-stiddle. It's absolutely brilliant. Brilliant!'

And so Gorbly came out, and said, 'Hello, Drodbar – I hear you've invented the ban-dan-bladder-stiddle – congratulations. Er – what exactly is it?' And Drodbar said, 'It's a wonderful device, that will revolutionize the world. It's very simple. It's just a round thing that's easy to push along, that's all.'

And then Gorbly went white, and said in a strangled voice, 'It hasn't by any chance got spokes in it, has it?' 'Yes, it has as a matter of fact,' said Drodbar, 'how the devil did you know?' And Gorbly said, 'That's not a ban-dan-bladder-stiddle, you stupid idiot, that's a wheel, and I invented it first – how dare you steal my idea?' And a great fight broke out between them, and if the man who invented fire hadn't come along and threatened to set light to them both they might have killed each other.

Anyway, there was a great dispute, and all the hairy old

Neanderthals met together at Stonehenge – a lovely place – to decide who really thought of it first. And eventually, after days and days of argument, they come to the conclusion that although it seemed likely that Drodbar thought of his ban-dan-bladder-striddle before Gorbly thought of his wheel, nevertheless they were going to give the credit to Gorbly because he thought of a much better name for it.

I think they were right, actually, I mean think of going into a garage and asking them to put a bit more air into your ban-dan-bladder-stiddle. Still, you can't help feeling sorry for poor old Drodbar, you know. He went into a great depression and went round mumbling and moaning about his wretched old ban-dan-bladder-stiddle – eventually he was run down by the world's first pterodactyl-drawn chariot. A terrible end.

I know lots of people who've thought of things just a little bit too late. Poor old Spotty Muldoon – he thought of splitting the atom the other day. If only he could have had the idea about thirty years ago. He'd have made a bloody fortune.

DUD AND PETE

The classic teaming of Dudley Moore – as the idiot who knows nothing – and Peter Cook – as the idiot who knows everything – dates from their BBC television series *Not Only But Also.* The sketches were semi-improvised, and the Pete and Dud characters have long outlived the original programmes. This sketch was first broadcast on 22 January 1966, in the second programme of the second series.

Disease

Dud is sitting up in bed with a thermometer in his mouth.

DUD *(indistinctly)*: Here. Pete – take this thermometer out of my mouth, will you?

PETE: Has it been in the full half-hour?

DUD: Yes.

PETE: Under the tongue?

DUD: Yes.

PETE: No cheating?

DUD: No, honestly.

PETE: You've not been breathing in rapidly and cooling it?

DUD: No, no.

PETE: All right, let's have a look. *(Takes the thermometer out.)* Oh dear, oh dear, oh dear.

DUD: What's it say, Pete?

PETE: It's ninety-eight degrees point four.

DUD: That's normal, isn't it?

PETE: That's normal, Dud – that's a dreadful thing to be at this time of the year. Very few people are normal at this time of the year. Should be about ninety-eight point three, is normal temperature.

DUD: I do hate having a cold, don't you? I mean, why does God have to plague us with germs and things?

PETE: How dare you say that! How dare you accuse God of plaguing you with germs – it's nothing of the sort – the germs are plagued by you far more. Do you know that germs were the first things to be invented? The first thing which was created was a germ.

DUD: Were they?

PETE: He said, 'Let there be germs', and there they were, millions of them, covering the face of the earth, having a wonderful time swimming about, going to picnics, having a marvellous time. And then after a few million years, God become a bit bored with the germs, being so small – couldn't see them from his lofty stance, you see – and so he invented the human being. And then the poor old germ had to start flying up people's nostrils and creeping all over the place – they don't like doing it, not one bit.

DUD: No, I'm sure they don't, actually. But there are a lot of them about, aren't there, Pete?

PETE: Well, they're omnipresent, Dud. Omnipresent.

DUD: They're in the air, they're in the bed, they're in your socks, they're everywhere . . . I mean, only the other day, Mr. Ripley, he sat on a germ-ridden radiator, and he contracted polaroids.

PETE: They're the things what develop in eight seconds, are they? Very quick-working disease, the worst kind. But you know, whatever you say about disease, it is a wonderful thing. Because if it wasn't for disease, and suffering, and all the ghastly tornados and things that happen like that, ordinary life wouldn't be happy. You wouldn't enjoy yourself when you're having a good time if you didn't have disease to fear and look back on.

DUD: Yes, that's true enough. Mind you, Pete, I've had my toll of disease.

PETE: Have you had your toll?

DUD: I've had my lot of suffering in this world, mate.

PETE: When did you have it?

DUD: Well, when I was three, Pete, I nearly died, you know.

PETE: I had no idea.

DUD: When I was a mere babe, my face was all blue, I could hardly breath, you know? And my Mum didn't know what was wrong, and Doctor Armstrong didn't know what was wrong, and nobody knew what was wrong . . . and finally a great surgeon found the solution to it all.

PETE: What was the cause of it?

DUD: The cause of the disease was my father holding me underwater for ten minutes.

PETE: A hereditary disease, was it?

DUD: That's right.

PETE: You know, in the family – there's a lot of those about.

DUD: But what I don't understand, Pete, is in this world of scientific advancement and technicological miracles, when man is reaching out into the unknown and into space with loony probes, is why there's no cure for the common cold.

PETE: Ah – the common cold *was* cured a few years back by Mr. Wainwright. Mr. Wainwright of Harlesden invented a cure for the common cold. He come across it in some fig jelly, a terrible mould of one kind or the other, so he wrote up to Boots about it, but during that same night, two burly men come from the British Handkerchief Association, and they bunged him two million pound in used notes, and he's off in the Bahamas now with some blonde floozy I dare say. He burnt his solution.

DUD: Yes, terrible that, ain't it? Mind you, you know, there are some wonderful cures about – I mean, I was reading in *Reveille* the other day, in the medical section, I read that the Chinese have got this wonderful system of agriculture.

PETE: No, it's *aquapuncture*, the science of the pin – and what a wonderful science that is.

DUD: What a wonderful science, Pete.

PETE: The Chinese – for example, if you got toothache in China, you ring up the Chinese doctor, all he comes round with is a little pin. That's all he has, in a black bag, you see; and he says, 'So you got toothache', takes out his pin, and with uncanny Chinese precision, Dud, he bangs it right into your lumbar regions.

DUD: Where's that, Pete?

PETE: Well, lumbar region is a technical medical word for the bum. So he bangs the pin in the bum, and of course you forget about the pain in your jaw, and you start thinking about the pain in your bum, Dud. Toothache gone – away dull care.

DUD: Yes, toothache gone, but bum-ache!

PETE: Now, what he does then, the Chinese doctor, before the ache can develop in the bum, bangs it in the knee, so you got knee-ache.

DUD: And then he goes round the body.

PETE: He goes round the whole body . . .

DUD: One step ahead.

PETE: One step ahead, as you say. And as soon as he's run out of the whole human body, then he gives the pin to the patient, and says, 'Go out and stick it in other people'. And you go out and stick it in other people, and get a good laugh when you see them jump up in the air, and you stop thinking about your own disease, and you start enjoying other people's. Best medicine, that.

DUD: Wonderful – mind you, we have some wonderful folk-cures our side of the Atlantic, you know Pete.

PETE: Oh, the gypsy cure.

DUD: Yes – as you know, my mum is a part-time gypsy.

PETE: She is a Romany, is she?

DUD: Yes, but she wasn't built in a day.

PETE: 'Course she wasn't, she took nine months like everyone else.

DUD: No, it's a joke Pete, never mind. No, when I used to get ear-ache . . .

PETE: Built in a day?

DUD: Built in a day, I'll tell you about it later. When I used to get ear-ache, when I was a mere suckling, and still at my mother's . . . breast . . . she used to pop a threepenny bit . . .

PETE: Where did she put the threepenny bit?

DUD: She used to put a threepenny bit under my pillow, and tie my ear to the door with a bit of string, and slam the door very hard.

PETE: What effect did this somewhat primitive treatment have on the ear, Dud?

DUD: It nearly tore my ear off.

PETE: And the door?

DUD: Well, the handle fell off.

PETE: Sounds like a rather useless cure.

DUD: Oh, it was, totally useless.

PETE: A useless folk-cure.

DUD: But mind you, I think half the complaints and diseases in the world are in the mind, you know.

PETE: That's where they have their origins, Dud, in the human mind, that's where it all begins. Psycho-pathetic things come up, and in the cerbaceous glands everything starts moving.

DUD: It's all in the mind.

PETE: Just tell yourself, 'I've not got a cold', and you won't have a cold.

DUD: Really?

PETE: Yes.

DUD: I have not got a cold.

PETE: There – you're cured.

DUD *(sneezes)*: I sneezed, Pete.

PETE: No, you didn't sneeze – you *thought* you sneezed. *(Dud sneezes again.)*

PETE: There, you thought you sneezed again, didn't you?

DUD: Yes.

PETE: Yes, well be careful – I don't want to catch your mind.

'THE GLUMS'

The horrific working-class Glum family – forerunners of Alf Garnett and his brood – have appeared on television in recent years; however they first appeared in the famous 1950s radio series, *Take It From Here*, which first established Frank Muir and Denis Norden as a brilliant writing team. This episode was first broadcast in the BBC Light Programme on 7 May 1958.

MR. GLUM	Jimmy Edwards
RON	Dick Bentley
ETH	June Whitfield
TED THE DOCTOR	Wallas Eaton

'A Saga of Sixpence'

Pub background noises.

TED: Time, Gentlemen, please! . . . Here, finish up . . . Mr. Glum, you've been knocking them back pretty steady tonight, ain't you?

MR. GLUM: No need to adopt that disapprobrious tone, Ted. The day you see drink get the better of me, that's the day you can pass remarks.

TED: No offence, Mr. Glum.

MR. GLUM: All right. Now, if you'll just help me up off the floor and point me vaguely towards south-east, I'll be on my way.

TED: Now now, don't leave bad friends. I'm just curious what occasioned this relaxation of your normal moderation.

MR. GLUM: Thank you for the credit, there. What do you think's the cause of it? What do you think, eh?

TED: I don't really know.

MR. GLUM: Ah dear . . . that boy of mine. My Ron. Now, take last Tuesday. Before you take it, take a Brown. Last Tuesday, there was Ron, with Eth, on the sofa, but acting so far-fetched Eth had to say something – she had to *say* something . . .

ORCHESTRA: 'RON AND ETH THEME', *heralding a flash-back.*

ETH: Oh, Ron . . . don't think I'm trying to pry, beloved, but is everything all right? I mean, the whole evening you've been sort of – wrought up . . . have you got anything at all on your mind?

RON: No, Eth.

ETH: Dearest, I don't want to appear to doubt your word, but . . . Ron, every time you think I'm not looking, you go over to the mirror and hit yourself on top of the head with a hammer. I think I'm entitled to ask why.

RON: My neck's too short.

ETH: You're fibbing, aren't you, Ron?

RON: Yes, Eth.

ETH: Unless you confide in me I can't help you, and I'm very worried about you. There's something behind this hitting yourself on top of the head with a hammer. Oh Ron – you're going to tell me whether you like it or not.

RON: All right, Eth.

ETH: Well?

RON: I don't like it, Eth. It hurts.

ETH: Then why keep doing it, dear heart?

RON: I've got to, Eth – it's the only way to solve my problem.

ETH: Ah – so there *is* a problem – I thought you wouldn't keep hitting yourself on top of the head with a hammer unless there was some sort of reason. Oh, dearest, won't you let me help you?

RON: If you like, Eth – here's the hammer.

ETH: Oh, not hit you, Ron – solve your problem.

RON: That *will* solve it, Eth. If I'm hit on top of the head with a hammer long enough, I won't have a problem.

ETH: You won't have a head, either. Ron Glum, you're going to tell me here and now what problem has made you take to hitting yourself on top of the head with a hammer. Is it a feeling of guilt?

RON: No, Eth.

ETH: Family troubles?

RON: No, Eth.

ETH: An affair of the heart?

RON: No, Eth.

ETH: Then what?

RON: I've got a sixpence stuck up my nose.

ETH: Oh, *Ron*!

ORCHESTRA: LINK.

MR. GLUM: There – hold his stupid head back, Eth. Let me shine the torch up his beak. We'll see if there's any . . . ah – yes – yes, I can see the tanner.

ETH: Which side is it?

MR. GLUM: Tails.

ETH: No, Mr. Glum – which side of his nose?

MR. GLUM: It's – er – the right-hand nostril. The starboard as you might say. Well, there's a thing, Eth. Oh, Ron, you are a reckless boy. Next time you're tossing a tanner for drinks, pull your head back!

ETH: That wasn't how he did it, Mr. Glum, it was – well *you* tell us, Ron.

RON: Well, Dad gave me a shilling to go and get him six pennorth of chips . . .

MR. GLUM: That's right, yes . . .

RON: . . . so I went to the fish shop, and the man gave me the chips and then a sixpence change. And then I remembered – Dad likes vinegar sprinkled over.

MR. GLUM: Yes – it gives the paper a better flavour. I still don't see why you put the sixpence in your nose.

RON: I should think that would have been obvious. How else could I pick up the vinegar bottle? I had the chips in one hand, and in the other hand I had the sixpence.

ETH: But – couldn't you have put it in your pocket?

RON: No, Eth, it's chained to the counter.

ETH: Oh, Ron – not the vinegar bottle – the sixpence! Why didn't you put the sixpence in your pocket?

RON: Eth – it's easy enough to be wise afterwards.

MR. GLUM: So what you're trying to say to us is that in order to handle the chips *and* the vinegar you shoved the tanner up your hooter!

RON: Yes, Dad.

MR. GLUM: Strike a flaming light. I suppose we should only be thankful that the change didn't come in six pennorth of coppers. How would you have distributed it then? Well, then what did you do when you'd got the sixpence up your conk, then?

RON: I walked home, and I gave you the chips, and you gave me one for going. And I ate it. Then I licked my fingers. First this finger, then that finger . . .

MR. GLUM: Yes, all right, all right, all right . . . never mind the human interest. Just give me the saline facts.

RON: Er . . . well. Oh – then I went upstairs and had me lie down . . . and when I woke up, I suddenly thought, 'Ooh! – what about Dad's sixpence?' You know, Eth, I looked everywhere for it . . .

ETH: You'd forgotten where you'd put it?

RON: Yes, Eth – and you'll never in a million years guess where I found it.

MR. GLUM: Up your great stupid conk.

RON: Ooh, Dad, you got it first time – it took me ages.

ETH: Mr. Glum, it's no good you just standing there staring at Ron with that expression of loathing. The thing's done. Now, what about your son?

MR. GLUM: *He's* going to be done very soon . . .

ETH: This is no time for recriminations, Mr. Glum. If we don't get that sixpence out, it might – well, I don't want to be an alarmist, but one must think of these things – the sixpence might work its way into the interior of

Ron's head.

MR. GLUM: That must be fascinating country! It's all very well to keep saying 'Get it aht, get it aht', Eth – but *how*?

ETH: How? Well, you never had any such difficulty getting sixpences out of the gas meter.

MR. GLUM: I do that from the back with a long bit of wire. This is different, Eth. 'Ere, wait a minute – of course I know how to dislodge it – it's a simple scientific principle.

ETH: How?

MR. GLUM: Hit him on top of the head with a hammer.

ETH: He's been doing that since last night – it doesn't work! Look – surely there must be some way of blowing it down?

MR. GLUM: Blowing it – well, I suppose that's worth trying – we could shove the nozzle of the bicycle pump into his ear, and then we could . . .

ETH: No! No, Mr. Glum, Ron'll blow it . . . look, beloved . . .

RON: Yes, Eth.

ETH: Now listen – place one finger tight against your good nostril, like this . . . (*Nasally.*) That's right . . .

RON (*nasally*): That's right . . .

ETH (*nasally*): . . . now blow as hard as you can down the sixpenny one . . . go on . . .

RON (*nasally*): Right . . .

ETH: Has anything happened, Mr. Glum?

MR. GLUM: Nothing's happened except he's taken on a startling resemblance to Louis Armstrong. All right, give over, Ron. Hold him up, Eth, his knees are sagging. Here – while he's half sparked out, give me hold of the sugar tongs . . . I'll try and see if I can get a purchase on the coin with them. Hold steady, Ron.

RON: Ow! No, Dad . . . ow!

MR. GLUM: Now don't make out that that hurt . . . what a baby you are. Eth, give me a hand trying to pull the sugar tongs down again. I must say I never imagined I'd get 'em up *that* far. There we are, that's extricated them. (*Ron groans.*)

MR. GLUM: All right, I'm sorry – if you'll just keep your head still this time I might get them up the *right* nostril.

ETH: No, Mr. Glum – no, no, no – I don't think you should.

MR. GLUM: And why not – he's my boy.

ETH: Yes, I know, but he's my boy too, and if it's going to be got down like that, then it should be done by – well, somebody qualified.

MR. GLUM: You mean a sweep?

ETH: A doctor. A proper doctor. Mr. Glum – you must ring up the hospital, and we'll go there right away.

ORCHESTRA: LINK.

DOCTOR: All right, Mr. Glum – as soon as I got your phone call I got the whole operating theatre staff standing by. So now tell me – what exactly is this 'startling challenge to modern surgery' that you mentioned?

MR. GLUM: Never mind the sarcasm, doctor, just sit down and conserve your strength for the task what lies ahead. I am a father, a proud father, who is putting all his faith in your professional skill. This here is Eth, here – a girl whose married future depends on the steadiness of your healing hands.

DOCTOR: And, er – who is this?

RON: I'm the one who put the money up.

DOCTOR: Put the money up?

MR. GLUM: Doctor, doctor, steel yourself – this young youth, standing there, outwardly so brave and unconcerned – doctor, the time for mincing words is past. He's got a sprazi up his snitch.

DOCTOR: A what up his what?

ETH: His nose – there's a sixpence up there.

DOCTOR: And for that you made me put the entire casualty wing on an emergency standby?

MR. GLUM: Doctor, forgive an old man's anxiety – I was speaking not only as a father of a boy, but as the owner of a sixpence.

DOCTOR: I've never heard of such a waste of . . . hello – operating theatre?

INTERCOM VOICE: Yes, doctor?

DOCTOR: Save your lights – and bring me a pair of tweezers. Now for goodness' sake, let's have a look at this nose . . . yes – yes, I see it . . . but what are these abrasions on the other nostril?

MR. GLUM: They're tong marks.

DOCTOR: Tong . . . you mean he's Chinese?

MR. GLUM: No, no, no – he always looks like that, it comes of not eating his greens. Doctor – I don't like the look in your eyes – is there any hope?

DOCTOR: Hope? To think I left a golfing dinner for this!

For heaven's sake get outside, you two, and let me get at this nose.

ORCHESTRA: LINK.

MR. GLUM: I still say the way that doctor spoke to me was most unprofessional. I got a good mind to report his whole attitude to the B.R.M.

ETH: Oh, Mr. Glum, it's over now. We're home . . . shut the door, Ron. The sixpence is out, so let's consider the episode closed.

MR. GLUM: Not quite closed – may I remind you, Eth, I'm still waiting for Ron to give me back me tanner.

ETH: For goodness' sake, Ron, give it back to him and let's have done.

RON: Right-ho, Eth. Er, now what did I do with it . . .

ETH: Oh Ron . . .

RON: I've got it Eth . . . I remember having it in my hand on the bus when the Inspector wanted to see my ticket, and I remember that I had my cap in one hand, and the sixpence in the other, and I had to get my ticket out. Now where did I put the sixpence?

ETH: Oh, Ron, Ron – you *didn't* . . .

RON: Oh, Eth, you don't think I'm so silly as to put it up my nose again after all that? I may not be very clever, but I don't make the same mistake twice.

MR. GLUM: Well where is it, then? Where is it? . . . Ron, Ron – I'm talking to you . . .

RON: Are you talking to me, Dad?

MR. GLUM: Of course I'm talking to you!!

RON: You'll have to speak up.

MR. GLUM: Speak up?!!

RON: It's funny, I don't seem to be able to hear out of this ear.

MR. GLUM: Oh, get the bent wire, get the tongs. . . .

'THE GOON SHOW'

'Caricatures against a background of fantasy' was one description given to the inhabitants of *The Goon Show*. Whereas in other radio shows actors simply play the roles in the story, in *The Goon Show* the three main performers play characters who then play the roles in the plot, so that the action works on three levels instead of two. Characters often meet as if for the first time in the course of a story; but asides, made *in character*, make it clear that they 'really' know each other, and are indeed 'only acting'. In this show, the cast go back to the days of ancient Rome; but beneath the togas, the familiar characters are just the same as always. This text is as broadcast, except that cuts, made for timing (or other) reasons, have been re-instated, and are shown in square brackets.

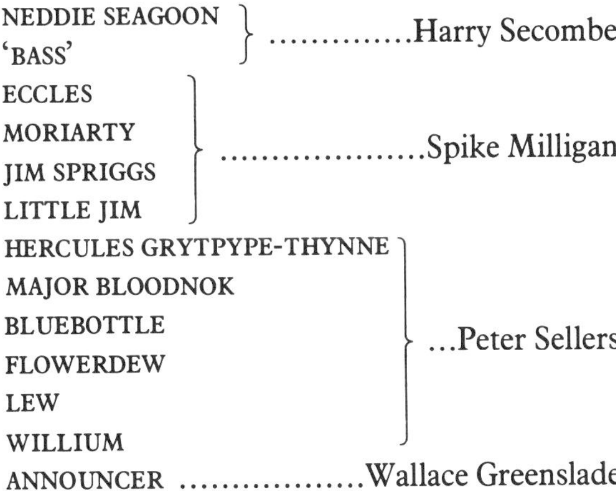

NEDDIE SEAGOON
'BASS' } ....Harry Secombe

ECCLES
MORIARTY
JIM SPRIGGS
LITTLE JIM } ....Spike Milligan

HERCULES GRYTPYPE-THYNNE
MAJOR BLOODNOK
BLUEBOTTLE
FLOWERDEW
LEW
WILLIUM } ...Peter Sellers

ANNOUNCER ....Wallace Greenslade

Script by Spike Milligan and Larry Stephens
First broadcast 28 March 1957 in the BBC Home Service

'The Histories of Pliny the Elder'

GREENSLADE: This is the BBC Home Service. History for Schools. Question One – How do you spell C–A–T?

HARRY: Cat! Well done!

GREENSLADE: Question Two – name two English Queens called Elizabeth.

HARRY: Jim.

GREENSLADE: Question Three – What is the Goon Show's first name and give an example of.

HARRY: That is a trick question, Wallace! And so here is a trick answer entitled: 'The Histories of Pliny the Elder'.

ORCHESTRA: ROMAN-STYLE FANFARE.

GRAMS: FADE UP SOUND OF SURF AND SEA-GULLS.

GREENSLADE: And so in the year X–L–one–one–one B. C., Julius Caesar set foot on the British shore and was greeted by the natives.

ECCLES: Hellooo!

THYNNE: Veni, vidi, vici.

ECCLES: Eh?

THYNNE: I came – I saw – I conquered.

ECCLES: Oooohh . . . fine! Fine. I'm just going in for a dip – give the old kippers a steam. *(Going off.)* Oh, I do like to be beside the seaside . . .

THYNNE: Brutus Moriartus, seize that Briton and prepare him for a life of slavery.

MORIARTY: Ave Caesar. Cave! Here comes another Charlie Britannicus.

BASS *(Harry: Northern)*: When you're tramp, tramp, tramping along the high road . . . *(Approaching.)* Hello folks . . . Who cares! . . .

THYNNE: Gad – he's up early.

MORIARTY: He must be one of the early Britons.

THYNNE *(aside)*: Quiet, you fumant Centurion. Tell the men to pull the galley ashore, quickly. *(Aloud.)* Ah, good morning!

BASS: 'Ow do! I see your boat's all loaded up. Going round the lighthouse?

THYNNE: By Jupiter, no! We're here on business. We've

come to conquer England.

BASS: Oh, have you? Well, they're all at breakfast at the moment.

THYNNE: We'll wait.

BASS: Well, you'll 'ave to take your place in the queue. We've got fixtures with the Vikings, the Danes and the Picts first. Wait a minute – 'ave you told anybody you're coming?

THYNNE: Veritas, no! We didn't know ourselves until after lunch. We were just passing and we thought we'd drop in and conquer you.

BASS: Oh! Well, I don't want to be rude, but I don't recognize the colours your lads are wearing.

MORIARTY: You savage English fool! This is the Imperial Caesar. We are Romans. Prepare yourself for combatus.

BASS: Righto . . . righto . . . I'll go and get our lads together. Only, being Sunday, they'll be in the pubs you know.

[MORIARTY: Caesar, shall I spear him?

THYNNE: Don't be a foolus Moriartus. Let him go. It will give us a chance to get our forces ashore.

BASS *(going)*: Right! Well, I'll go and tell our chief, Britannicus.]

ORCHESTRA: BLOODNOK LINK.

BLOODNOK: Ooooogh! The Romans want to take the field against us, do they?

BASS: That's right, Britannicus. They're very keen to 'ave a do with us, you know. And you never know – we might win!

BLOODNOK: Win? No, we mustn't – we don't want to spoil our record.

BASS: Well, what'll I tell them, then?

BLOODNOK: Well, tell 'em to put their goal on the edge of the cliffs. That'll give their goalie a bit of a rough time. Ooughghgh!

BASS: Ha ha! – You don't care, do you. Righto – kick-off two-thirty, then.

BLOODNOK: Splendid.

ORCHESTRA: MUTED TROMBONES AS PER ROMAN WAR-HORNS.

GREENSLADE: And so the Britons in their woad took the field before the might of the Roman Army.

GRAMS: WEMBLEY FOOTBALL CROWD [SINGING LAST PART OF 'LAND OF HOPE AND GLORY' –

THEN] CHEERING. FADE UNDER.

THYNNE: Brutus Moriartus – here! What kind of Army is this that takes the field in blue jerseys with a ball at their feet?

MORIARTY: It must be some kind of trickus. Look! They're forming up.

EFFECTS: REFEREE'S WHISTLE.

THYNNE: That must be their signal to attack.

MORIARTY: Forward, men! Advancus!

GRAMS: MIX CHARGE AND SOUND OF BATTLE WITH CHEERING FOOTBALL CROWD. FADE UNDER.

BLOODNOK: I say! They're a rough lot these Romans.

EFFECTS: WHISTLE.

MORIARTY: What's this? What have we stopped for?

BASS: Rough play, that's what we've stopped for, I'll tell the . . . Every time I come up the wing your outside right swipes at me with a dirty big sword.

THYNNE *(approaching)*: I say, what's all this hold-up about?

BASS: Rough play. We don't hold with all this javelin practice when the ball's in play. And another thing – you're only allowed eleven men on the field. I've counted six hundred and ninety-three of yours so far.

THYNNE: All right – I'll send one off.

BASS: Righto! Play on!

GRAMS: BATTLE STARTS AGAIN AS BEFORE. FADE UNDER.

GREENSLADE: The result – Romans nine hundred – England three. War stopped play.

GRAMS: MARCHING FEET. MEN WHISTLING 'LILLI MARLENE' OVER. FADE DOWN AND UNDER.

PETER: Like a mighty octopus, the legions of Rome spread across England. For ten years Caesar ruled with an iron hand – then with a wooden foot – and finally with a piece of string. How much of this could Britain take?

ORCHESTRA: FADE IN HARP ARPEGGIOS ACCOMPANYING SPIKE.

SPIKE: Oh Caesar – I come to sing melodies divine to you.

THYNNE: Sing on, oh proud minstrel.

SPIKE: Thank you. *(Sings.)* Caesar is a noble man – a king of great renown – a gentleman every inch of him – from his feet to his hair of brown.

THYNNE: Moriartus – this man is a bit of a crawler. Why does he follow such a profession, Moriartus?

MORIARTY: For money, Caesar. He tells me he wants to die rich.

THYNNE: And so he shall. Give him this sack of gold and then strangle him.

MORIARTY: Yes, Caesar. *(Strangling noises, off.)* I see that ten years in Britain have not changed your imperial Roman outlook, Caesar.

THYNNE: True, Moriartus; always a Roman, I.

MORIARTY: Will you take wine?

THYNNE: No thanks – I think I'll have a half of mild and a packet of crisps.

GRAMS: FADE IN NOISE OF APPROACHING RABBLE.

GREENSLADE: Caesar – Caesar . . .

THYNNE: Oh! It's Stomachus Grossus.

GREENSLADE: Caesar, there is an angry rabble outside. We have their leader captive.

THYNNE: Is he bound?

GREENSLADE: Of his health I know naught, sir.

THYNNE: Bring him hither.

OMNES: STRUGGLE.

EFFECTS: CHAINS RATTLING.

BLOODNOK: Take your hands off me! Do you want to catch something? Ahh – so you're Julius Caesar, yes?

MORIARTY: Caesar is all things to all men.

BLOODNOK: Oh, it must be hell in there! Look, Mr. Caesar, we've just discovered why you've been here ten years. You've conquered us.

MORIARTY: Well?

BLOODNOK: Well, get out! . . . I mean, get out! Or we'll ban mid-week matches – and mid-week cigarettes as well.

GREENSLADE: Beware, Britannicus Bloodnokus – the Gods are angry.

BLOODNOK: I know – I've just been hit by a rotten tomato. Oh, the bird, the bird!

MORIARTY: Why, don't you stop him, Julius Caesar?

BLOODNOK: How can I, when I'm playing the part of Bloodnok?

MORIARTY: Now listen – for this rebellion, Bloodnokus, you'll be thrown to the wolves.

BLOODNOK: Not that team! No! I'm a London man.

GREENSLADE: Good Britannicus, you have one alternative.

You will be freed providing you give us four good men for the Coliseum games in Rome.

BLOODNOK: Yes! – I've got some likely English charlies who would suit you perfectly. They were very successful at the Scottish games.

MORIARTY: Did they do well?

BLOODNOK: Very well – they managed to get away with their lives.

MORIARTY: Very well. Deliver those men to Caesar's Royal Barge at X–X–I–X–X–I–and-a-half hours tomorrow.

BLOODNOK: I'll do that. Here's the first one – Max Geldraysus.

MAX GELDRAY AND ORCHESTRA: 'GET HAPPY'.

ORCHESTRA: ROMAN SEA-LINK.

GRAMS: SEA SOUNDS – CREAKING OARS.

GREENSLADE: And so, some months later, a Roman slave-galley drew nigh to Ostia.

GRAMS: BRING UP CREAKING OF OARS BRIEFLY.

ELLINGTON *(off)*: In . . . Out . . . In . . . Out . . .

ECCLES: Make up your mind!

BLUEBOTTLE: Have you ever rowed a gallery before, Ecculus?

ECCLES: Is that what we're doing?

BLUEBOTTLE: Yes.

ECCLES: No, I've never done this before.

ELLINGTON: Faster, you dogs!

BLUEBOTTLE: He wants our dogs to go faster.

ELLINGTON: Silence, you scum!

ECCLES: He wants our scum to go silent.

EFFECTS: CRACK OF WHIP.

ELLINGTON: Do you want a taste of the lash?

BLUEBOTTLE: No thanks – I've just had some cocoa.

ECCLES: Oh, look! They're bringing a new slave from the reserves.

BLUEBOTTLE: Goody!

EFFECTS: RATTLING OF CHAINS.

SEAGOON *(approaching)*: Let me go, you devils! How dare you? Take your hands off me! *(Etc. etc.)*

OMNES: MURMURINGS OF 'SHUT UP', 'WELSH DOG', ETC. ETC.

SEAGOON: How dare you chain me to this oar? I shall write to the *Times* about this – in print! [I know a Welsh M.P. who'll do anything for publicity.]

FLOWERDEW: Oh, shut up! It was perfectly quiet till you came along! You're not the only man chained to the oars, you know.

SEAGOON: Now listen to me, all of you.

FLOWERDEW: All of me *is* listening to you.

SEAGOON: I am the Welsh chieftain Caractacus Seagoon. I, for one, will never surrender to the might of Rome. I'll fight them up hill and down Mrs. Dale.

ECCLES: Wait a minute! How did they take you prisoner, then?

SEAGOON *(annoyed)*: I was in the bath. The one day a year they could catch me with my socks off.

ECCLES: It must have been hell in there.

BLUEBOTTLE: What are we going to do, then, Caractacus? How can we file through these chains?

SEAGOON: How? *(Hushed.)* How? This evening I received a cake from a friend. And guess what's inside?

BLUEBOTTLE: You mean there's . . .

SEAGOON: Yes. Raisins!

[BLUEBOTTLE: Ooh! I thought you were going to say a file.

SEAGOON: So did the listeners. *(Laughs.)*

ECCLES: *I* didn't think there was going to be a file inside.]

ELLINGTON *(off)*: Stop that talking at the back there.

BLUEBOTTLE: It wasn't me, sir! It was Harold Prott.

EFFECTS: CRACK OF WHIP.

BLUEBOTTLE: Oohhh! You flicked my knee.

ORCHESTRA: BRIEF SEA THEME.

OMNES *(over)*: NAUTICAL SHOUTS.

GREENSLADE: That night the galley docked at Ostia, and the slaves were put up for auction.

SPIKE: All right. Now then, come on now. What am I bid for these three British-type slaves? Ecculus – a lovely piece of property – claims to be descended from his father. No bids? Come on – anybody?

SEAGOON: Three dinas!

SPIKE: You fool – you're up for sale as well. There you are – a chap with initiative. All right then – what about this last one? A pair of genuine English knees with a hat attached, called Bluebottelus. Can tie knots, rub two sticks together and kill his grandmother.

LEW: I'll bid ten thousand dinas the three!

SPIKE: Sold!

LEW: This way lads . . . I seen 'im, I seen 'im . . .

SEAGOON: I say, this is dashed decent of you to buy us.

Who are you?

LEW: Me? I do all the bookings for the Colosseum. I seen 'em . . .

SEAGOON: You seen them, eh . . . The Coliseum? Could you get us a couple of tickets?

LEW: You won't need any.

SEAGOON: Oh! What's on?

LEW: *You* are.

SEAGOON: Am I?

LEW: Yes – tonight.

SEAGOON: Oh! I'd better get the old Hobson's choice going, hadn't I. *(Sings:)* We'll keep a welcome in the – *(Aside.)* I've done the Palladium, you know *(Sings.)* – iiiiin the hillside! Mi-mi-mi-mii! . . . *(Etc.)*

LEW: Lovely! Lovely, lovely . . . now try shouting 'help'.

SEAGOON: Heeelllpp!

LEW: Marvellous. That'll come in very useful.

ORCHESTRA: TWO OR THREE DRAMATIC DESCENDING CHORDS.

LEW: Right, now, you wait in there, boys. I'll tell you when it's your turn to go on. It'll be all right.

EFFECTS: IRON DOOR CLANGS SHUT.

SEAGOON: I say – what a wonderful fellow that agent is. My first night in Rome and I've got a booking already. Ah, now, let's have a look at this programme.

ECCLES: Oh! It's a good programme.

BLUEBOTTLE: What is the top of the bill?

SEAGOON: Oh, it's got a lovely opening act – 'Captive East Finchley boy scout will fight four starving lions'.

BLUEBOTTLE: Ooohhhhh! I do not like this lion game!

SEAGOON: You coward, Bluebottle. Face it like a man.

BLUEBOTTLE: Yes? Well, look at the encore there – 'Caractacus Seagoon will be strangled by a gorilla'.

SEAGOON: Heeelllpp! Let me out! You can't do this to me! I'm a British subject! I shall write to *The Times* about this! Help! Let me out! Heeeeellllpp!

FLOWERDEW: Oh, shut up! It was perfectly quiet until you came along.

SEAGOON: It's all right for you! You're a sailor – and sailors don't care!

FLOWERDEW: OoooOOHH!

SEAGOON: Now don't panic, everybody. I've got a plan. We'll overpower the guard.

BLUEBOTTLE: Yes!

ECCLES: Right! I'll take my boots off!

SEAGOON: Good! Now we'll get the boys and make our way down to the Tiber.

ECCLES: What's the Tiber?

SEAGOON: Half past dider *(nine)*.

PETER: That's what they want!

SEAGOON: I don't wish to know this . . . please . . . I say, kindly leave the prison *(Etc.)*. Ssh! Here comes the guard now.

EFFECTS: PRONOUNCED OPENING OF BOLTS AND IRON DOOR OPENS. TREMENDOUS WHACK.

GREENSLADE: *(Moan, fading off quickly.)*

SEAGOON: Right! Run for it!

GRAMS: FAST RUNNING FOOTSTEPS ON ECHO FADING OFF, SPEEDED UP.

GREENSLADE: [Dear Listeners, I thought you would like to know that the groan of pain you heard just now was not done by a Roman soldier but by me. And I thought I did it jolly well. I'm sure you all feel the better for knowing that.] Thank you. And now, Ray Ellingbaum.

RAY ELLINGTON QUARTET: YOU MADE ME LOVE YOU/THIS CAN'T BE LOVE.

ORCHESTRA: ROMAN LINK.

GREENSLADE: Through the catacombs, our heroes managed to reach the great water-pipe that runs under the Via Appia, known, of course, in the Army, as the famous Appia Pipe.
(Slight echo.)

SEAGOON: All right, lads. I think we're safe now. Ohh – wait a minute – look . . .

ECCLES: There's a man-hole cover right over us.

SEAGOON: Shine the beam of this candle on it.

ECCLES: Right.

SEAGOON: I'll push it off. Eccles, stand on my shoulders and pull me up.

ECCLES: Okay. *(Great effort.)* I'd like to see them do *this* on television.

OMNES: VERY PRONOUNCED CORNY GRUNTINGS.

BLUEBOTTLE: Shall I put the mange-hole cover back now, otherwise if it rains the hole will get wet.

SEAGOON: No. Leave it open. We don't want to lose the place – Shhh! Behind these bushes – someone's coming!

GRAMS: FOOTSTEPS APPROACHING. PAUSE.

SPLASH.

LITTLE JIM: He's fallen in the wa-ter!

SEAGOON: Little Jim! Little Jim . . . *(Etc.)* Thank you again.

WILLIUM: Ohhhhh, mate! Help me!

SEAGOON: Grab my hand, foot, ear, nose and teeth . . . Huppp!

WILLIUM: Oh! I didn't see that 'ole, you know . . . you don't see 'em on the corners, you know.

SEAGOON: Are you a Roman?

WILLIUM: No, mate, in the gloaman . . . My name's 'Annibal. You seen any elephants runnin' down the road?

SEAGOON: Elephants? You must be General Hannibal of Carthage.

WILLIUM: No, mate, I'm Willium Hannibal. I looks after the elephants in the Colosseum, there. I'm a Battersea slave, mate, there.

SEAGOON: How did you get captured?

WILLIUM *(aside)*: There's a lovely little boy.

LITTLE JIM: Get away, nasty man.

WILLIUM *(to Seagoon)*: Well, it were my Saturday off and I was taking the dog for a ball – and this Roman fellow come up and says, 'Take your 'at off'. And I does, and he said, 'That's a nasty lump on your bonce', and I said, 'Where?', and he said 'There', and pointed it out with a dirty great club. Oh, mate, ohhh. . . . When I come to, I feel me nut, an' he was right. There *was* a dirty big lump on it. But it was too late by then, you see – I was carrying buckets for the elephants at the Colosseum.

SEAGOON: But we are English-type slaves, too. Would you care to join us?

WILLIUM *(deliberately)*: Why? Are you coming apart?

SEAGOON: What's the year?

WILLIUM: 49 B.C.

SEAGOON: That proves how old that gag is.

ECCLES: It proves how old you are too. Haha ha!

GRAMS: SPLASH.

LITTLE JIM: He's fallen in the wa-ter again.

SEAGOON: *Now* you can put the lid on.

WILLIUM: I tell you what, mate. A lot of our lads joined an escaped gladiola called Sprartacus from Prortugal . . . he comes only from Prortugal, Sprartacus . . .

SEAGOON: Where is he?

WILLIUM: He's hidin' in the 'ole at the top of Vesemooverus.

SEAGOON: Let's to him!

ORCHESTRA: MUTED SOUND OF ROMAN HORNS.

GRAMS: THREE PEOPLE APPROACHING ON ROCKY ROAD.

SPRIGGS: Halt! Who goes there? Who goes the-ere?

SEAGOON *(off)*: Escaped British slaves.

SPRIGGS: Advance and be recognized . . . rec-og-nized.

SEAGOON: I am Caractacus Seagoon. I come from Wales.

SPRIGGS: I can see you don't come from sardines, Jim. I'll take you to Spartacus, the gladiola. Follow me.

GRAMS: WALKING ON ROCKY ROAD.

[SEAGOON: I say! There's a lot of lava around here.

SPRIGGS: Yes. It's from the last Vesuvius eruption. Covered the territory in lava.

SEAGOON: I see. So Spartacus is hiding in the lava-territory.

SPRIGGS: Yes indeed. Yes in-deed.] I'll knock.

EFFECTS: KNOCK ON DOOR.

BLOODNOK *(muffled)*: Just a minute, don't come in, please . . . I'm just changing my knees. Ooohhhh oohhhhh! Right!

EFFECTS: DOOR OPENS.

BLOODNOK: Now! Oohh!

SEAGOON: Britannicus Bloodnokus! How did you get to Italy?

BLOODNOK: Ask the writers. I've no idea.

SEAGOON: You are Spartacus?

BLOODNOK: Yessus – I was forced to change me name, you see. I fell out with Caesar.

SEAGOON *(horrified)*: You fell out with Caesar? How did that happenus?

BLOODNOK: We were in a chariot and we hit a bump in the road! Oghgh!

ECCLES: It was me!

SEAGOON: Come on, I want the trith and nothing but the troth.

BLOODNOK: Well, the trith is – how can I put it? You know that saying 'Caesar's wife is above suspicion'?

SEAGOON: Yes.

BLOODNOK: Well, I've put an end to all that rubbish. What a little beauty. [*(Sings.)* The laays of ancient Rome. . . .]

SEAGOON: Are we safe here?

BLOODNOK: Safe? My dear lad, we're actually *inside* the crater of an extinct volcano.

SEAGOON: Thank Heaven! Safe at last!

GRAMS: BUBBLING.

SEAGOON: I say, chaps . . . I say, look . . . look . . .

BLOODNOK: Oooohhh!

GRAMS: VOLCANO ERUPTS. PRE-RECORDING OF SCREAMS AND SHOUTS OF SEAGOON, BLUEBOTTLE, BLOODNOK, ECCLES AND SPRIGGS FLYING UP INTO AIR. FADE DOWN.

GREENSLADE: Next week, History for Schools tells the story of 'The Last Days of Pompeii'.

HARRY: Well, is that the lot for the old series, there, Wallace?

GREENSLADE: Yes.

HARRY: Right! Round the back for the old brandy, there!

GRAMS: RUNNING FOOTSTEPS.

ORCHESTRA: 'LUCKY STRIKE'.

GREENSLADE *(over music)*: That was the last of the present series of the Goon Show, a BBC recorded programme featuring Peter Sellers, Harry Secombe and Spike Milligan with the Ray Ellington Quartet, Max Geldray, and the Orchestra conducted by Wally Stott. Script by Spike Milligan and Larry Stephens. Announcer Wallace Greenslade. Bobby Jaye has been on the mixing panel, and the special effects were supplied by Ian Cook and Ron Belchier. The production was by Pat Dixon.

ORCHESTRA: SIG UP TO END.

JOYCE GRENFELL

Apart from her many films and her appearances on the television panel game *Face The Music*, Joyce Grenfell will be remembered for her monologues. They presented a range of characters – some of them serious – following the tradition of artists such as Ruth Draper. The most popular were those set in a nursery school, with its collection of exasperating infants – including the egregious George.

'Story Time'

Children! Pay attention, please! Now, free-time's over, so put away your things – we're going to tell our nice story, so come over here and make a circle on the floor all round me, and we're going to tell the story together – and today, we've got a visitor! So we can tell our story to her – now, come along – don't push! Now just take it gently. (Will you be all right there, Mrs. Binton? I think you get quite a good view of the proceedings.) Now hurry up, everybody, hurry up, there's lots of room for us all. (This group story-telling is quite a feature of our work here in the nursery school, Mrs. Binton – we like to feel that each little individual has a contribution to make to the world of make-believe, and of course many valuable lessons can be learned from team-work. Oh yes, we're a very happy band of brothers here.) – Edgar, let go of Timmy's ear, and sit down.

Now come along – now Sidney, come out from under the table, and join in the fun. . . . No, you're not in a space-rocket. . . . No, you can't wait for the count-down, now come on out *now*. Don't you want to help us tell our nice story? . . . Well then say no *thank* you, and stop machine-gunning people, please. Neville – Neville, finish being a train, dear, and sit down. . . . All right, well get into the station and then sit down.

George . . . don't do that.

Now, we'll have some nice straight backs, shall we? What are we going to tell our story about today? Rachel . . . take your shoe off your head, and put it on your foot. Now, shall we tell it about a little mouse, or what about a big red bus? . . . About a dear little bunny-rabbit? Well, Peggy, that *is* a good idea. We'll tell it about a dear little bunny-rabbit. No, Sidney, he wasn't a cowboy-bunny . . . and he didn't have a gun, now why don't you come out from under the table, and then you can help us tell the story. All right, stay there if you want to, but stop machine-gunning people, and I don't want to have to say that again. (He is one of our individualists, I'm afraid. He has *little* personality problems of aggression, but we feel that when his energies are canalized in the right direction he's going to be a very worthwhile person – that's our *hope*.)

Now – where did our bunny-rabbit live? . . . No, *not* in a TV set . . . *not* in a tree – no, *not* in a flat. Now *think*, please – *yes*, Hazel, he *did*, he lived in a hole! Of course. Only some of us call it a burrow, don't we? And he lived in a burrow, with – who? . . . His mummy-bunny-rabbit, yes, and – his daddy-bunny-rabbit, yes! And who else? . . . All his little brother-and-sister-bunny-rabbits – *wasn't* that nice! Yes it was, Sidney. . . . No, he wasn't a burglar-bunny-rabbit . . . no, nor was his daddy. Well, he was just an ordinary businessman-bunny-rabbit.

David – David, don't wander away like that . . . Yes, I *know* the window is over there, but you don't want to look out of it now, do you . . . oh, no – our story's getting *much* too exciting. Come and sit down by Ne-Neville . . . Neville! Don't pull your jersey down over your knees like that, please . . . well, because you get it all out of shape, and Mummy won't like that, will she? . . . Lavinia! Don't – Children! David . . . I don't want everybody pulling their jerseys down over their knees!

Now then . . . Peggy, you tell us – what was our bunny-rabbit's name? . . . Yes, I know his name was bunny-rabbit, but what did his mummy call him? . . . Well, 'piggy-bunny' isn't a *very* good name for a bunny-rabbit . . . you see, a piggy is a piggy, and a bunny is a bunny, so we can't have a piggy-bunny, can we? . . . No, nor a pussy-bunny . . . nor a doggy-bunny . . . nor an elephant-bunny, now let's be sensible, please. No, Sidney, 'Silly Old Fat Man' *isn't* a good name for a bunny-rabbit . . . and it isn't as funny as all that, there's no need to roll about on the floor.

Timmy . . . Timmy – what *have* you got in your hand? . . . But we haven't had toast and marmalade for two days . . . where did you find it? In your *pocket*? – Oh *no*, dear, you can't eat it, it's all fuzzy . . . Now look don't touch anything – just go and put it in the waste-paper basket and then wash your hands – Peggy, open the door for him – don't touch anything! Don't touch anything – just wash, and hurry back, because we need you. (Oh, dear!)

Now then, Hazel, what would you like our bunny-rabbit to be called? . . . Yes, I think 'Princess Anne' is a *lovely* name, but – I don't think it's a very good name for a *boy* bunny-rabbit, so we'll call him Bobby Bunny-rabbit – well, because it's his name – well, because I happen to know – look, we're not going to discuss it any more.

George . . . don't do that.

Lavinia – now, you tell us what our bunny rabbit was doing . . . He was riding a horse, was he? Oh, what an *unusual* thing for a rabbit! (They think of such original things, Mrs. Binton.)

Well, I expect he was going gallopy-gallopy, wasn't he . . . Oh good, Sidney, come out and help us tell about how – no, you can't *go* gallopy-gallopy . . . Sidney, come here . . . Sidney – children, you can't all go gallopy . . . this is *not* gallopy-gallopy time! . . .

(You know, Mrs. Binton, sometimes I don't think love is *enough* with children.)

TONY HANCOCK

The most important contribution that Hancock and his scriptwriters Simpson and Galton made to radio comedy was in moving it away from an atmosphere which was not so much fantasy as simply unreal (and in which any excuse for a joke would serve) to a world which was not too much exaggerated from reality, and in which the humour arose naturally out of the situations. This can be heard happening in 'Hancock's Half-Hours' – in earlier shows unlikely things happen such as Sid James stealing Waterloo Bridge or Nelson's column; by the fifth series the shows were much more natural. This one is only slightly exaggerated from what just might happen in real life.

With Tony Hancock, Sidney James, Bill Kerr, and Hattie Jacques as Miss Pugh. Policeman and Judge played by Kenneth Williams; Second Policeman played by Alan Simpson.

First Broadcast on 1 April 1958 in the BBC Light Programme.

'Hancock's Car'

GRAMS: SIGNATURE TUNE.

ANNOUNCER: We present Tony Hancock, Sidney James, Bill Kerr, Hattie Jacques and Kenneth Williams in. . . .

HANCOCK: H-H-Hancock's Half-Hour.

GRAMS: SIGNATURE TUNE.

HANCOCK: Now then – where shall we start? There's three of us – it shouldn't take long.

SID: You got a nerve – inviting me round for a drink and then roping me in to help clean your car.

HANCOCK: Well, it takes Bill and I too long. Six arms are better than four.

BILL: Well don't you think you're overdoing it, Tub? A car only needs polishing once a week, not every day.

HANCOCK: We live in a smoky atmosphere – look at this – a thin layer of smog all over it. Hullo, who's been writing messages on the bonnet with their fingers? 'Ernie Biggs loves Elsie Spurgeon'. I know that Ernie Biggs – he's the same one that runs along my fence with a stick of chalk. Wait till he comes home from school – I'll hide behind the hedge, I'll jump out on him, and I'll wrap his catapult round his neck. I will not have spotty-faced kids defacing my limousine! Go on – wash it off. I want the chrome and the paint-work shining so that you can see your face in it.

SID: I never known anyone so finicky about their car as you are. I haven't cleaned *my* car for three years.

HANCOCK: That is only so that any witnesses won't be able to tell what colour it was. It's a disgrace, your car is – you have to feel along the door to find where the handle is. I'm not letting mine get in a state like that. I'm *proud* of my car. It's the cleanest down this street. Dead elegant, this.

SID: Yeah, I've seen you – sitting up there all day at your bedroom window with a feather duster in your hand – and as soon as you see a speck of dust land, you're down! Buckets of water, polish, chamois leathers, hoses, vacuum cleaners – then back upstairs again, waiting for the next bit to land. It's an obsession.

HANCOCK: It is not. If I keep it in good nick, I stand to make more money on it if I ever decided to sell it. It's very difficult keeping a car clean down Railway Cuttings, all those trains going by. And they do it deliberately, I've watched them.

SID: Watched who?

HANCOCK: Those drivers. They see me cleaning the car, and they deliberately slow down, wait till the wind's in the right direction, then whoosh! – a funnel full of dirty black smoke comes hurtling over. And more than once I have had occasion to complain to British Railways about them heaving lumps of coal at it! I think they must be running a sweep down at the shunting yards – 'Let's see how many times we can hit 'Ancock's car!' It's no joke.

SID *(pointedly)*: It's kept *you* in fires since you bought it.

HANCOCK: That is not the point. A great lump of Welsh anthracite bouncing off it doesn't do the bonnet any good. Now come on, the sooner we start, the . . . I'll kill that next door's cat!

BILL: *Now* what's wrong?

HANCOCK: Look what he's done! Look what he's done! Horrible great paw-marks over the bonnet, up the window, across the roof and down the boot. He'll get *my* boot if I catch him again. Great ugly thing he is.

SID: Oh, come on, if we've got to do it, let's get it over with.

HANCOCK: Right – Bill, you get under the car and polish it. Sid—

BILL: Just a minute – did you say *under* the car?

HANCOCK: Yes, I did. I want the springs and all the stuff underneath polished right up. I want it shining – go on, crawl under there, you ratbag.

BILL: But Tub, what's the point? Nobody sees *under* the car.

HANCOCK: They do at the garage when it goes up on the ramp. I don't want them to look underneath my car and say 'Ooh, isn't it dirty!' I'm not all outward show, you know. I'm not like those women who just dust round the ornaments. Underneath, mate! – Then you can lift the bonnet up and polish the engine.

BILL *(ironically)*: Shall I take the tyres off and wash the inner tubes?

HANCOCK: Yes, you can do that afterwards. Then you can let the air out and put some fresh in. I want it looking just like it did when it came out of the showroom. Right

– to work!

GRAMS: MUSIC LINK.

HANCOCK: There – let's have a look – oh, that's a bit better, isn't it.

SID: It ought to be – blimey, three-and-a-half hours of continual rubbing. I swear my right arm's three inches shorter than the other.

HANCOCK: If a job is worth doing, it is worth doing well. Look at it gleaming there.

SID: Yeah. I still don't like the colour scheme, and I never have.

HANCOCK: Don't like the colour scheme? Orange and heliotrope? Very voguey, that is.

SID: I think it's the tartan hood that spoils it.

HANCOCK: You've got no taste, have you? You've got to have something bright for the hood to balance up with the pink-wall tyres.

SID: All you want is a couple of plants in there, and it'll look like a travelling coffee bar. Is it clean enough for you?

HANCOCK: It'll do for now. We'll have another three hours on it tomorrow. Bill – have you finished the underneath? Where is he?

SID: His legs are poking out the other side.

HANCOCK: I'll bet he's asleep. I've a good mind to jump on his ankles. I'd love to see him spring up and hit his head on the big end. Or, shall I start the engine up? His ear'ole's right by the end of the exhaust pipe. No, no, no, no, no, – ha ha! – no, no, no! Hang on, hang on – *(Shouts.)* Pull your legs in, there's a bus coming!

BILL: What – where – what – *(Bonk!)* Ow! Ow!

HANCOCK *(laughs)*: Oh dear – I did enjoy that! I bet his knees felt that! He didn't half fetch them a whack on that running board. . . . My running board! If you've damaged that running board you will have the benefit of my starting handle across your nose.

BILL: I haven't hurt your running board.

MISS PUGH: Coo-ee! Dinner's ready!

HANCOCK: We'd better go in now, otherwise she'll eat it all. Put a barrage balloon over the car in case it rains, William.

MISS PUGH: You must all be very hungry after all that work you've done – I've made a nice big dishful of cauliflower cheese.

HANCOCK: Oh – I don't like cauliflower cheese.

BILL: Neither do I.

SID: Neither do I.

MISS PUGH *(innocently)*: Don't you really?

HANCOCK: You *know* we don't like cauliflower cheese! You've always known it!

MISS PUGH: Oh, well, never mind – I'll just have to eat it all myself.

HANCOCK: You planned that! You made it on purpose – you're always doing that! You've made a list of everything we don't like, and you deliberately go and make dirty great binfuls of it. Ooh, you gannet!

MISS PUGH: You can have bread and dripping.

HANCOCK: Thank you very much indeed. The perfect Sunday dinner – roast bread and dripping. Most appetizing – the height of luxury. Draw the curtains – I don't want the neighbours looking in and seeing a man of my calibre eating bread and dripping.

SID: Turn it up, Grizzly, you must have something else in there.

MISS PUGH: No – there's no more.

HANCOCK: She's hidden it all! She buries it somewhere – she's like something out of Armand and Michaela Denis. She drags it all off to her lair and stands guard over it.

MISS PUGH: The car looks nice.

HANCOCK: Don't change the subject. Bread and dripping!

BILL: I'm hungry after all that work – I think I'll *have* some cauliflower cheese.

SID: Yes, I might as well, too.

MISS PUGH: But you don't like it! You said you didn't like it – you told me you didn't!

HANCOCK: Aha! That's frightened her! She didn't expect that! I'll have some too! Ha ha ha! It's worth making yourself ill just to see her face! Drops two inches every spoonful we take! Where's me blindfold – I can't look at it *and* eat it.

FX: DOORBELL RINGS.

HANCOCK: Miss Pugh – the front door!

MISS PUGH: Oh yes, right you are.

HANCOCK: No need to take your cauliflower cheese with you – we're not going to pinch it.

MISS PUGH: All right, but I know *exactly* how much is there.

HANCOCK: Oh, go and open the door.

FX: DOOR OPENS.

POLICEMAN: Good afternoon, Ma'am.

MISS PUGH: Oh, good afternoon, constable. Mr. Hancock – it's a policeman.

(Sid chokes.)

HANCOCK: Quick, slap Sid on the back, he's swallowed his cauliflower. It's all right, Sid, boy – he's not after *you*.

SID: Blimey. I know he don't want me – I haven't done anything for weeks. Just when I hear the word 'copper' – turns my stomach right over. I'll be all right in a minute.

HANCOCK: Won't you come in, constable? Anything I can do for you? Have some cauliflower cheese?

POLICEMAN: No thank you, sir, I'm on duty.

HANCOCK: Well, put some in your helmet for after.

POLICEMAN: Very kind of you, sir, but I'd rather not.

HANCOCK: You're very wise. What can I do for you?

POLICEMAN: Is that your car parked outside?

HANCOCK: Yes, that's right – magnificent vehicle, isn't she? Everybody round here admires her. Wonderful condition she's in.

POLICEMAN: Move it.

HANCOCK: Pardon?

POLICEMAN: *Move* it.

HANCOCK: Move it? *Move* it? Have you taken leave of your senses?

POLICEMAN: The aforementioned vehicle is causing an obstruction. Move it.

HANCOCK: Oh, come now, my good man – I live here – it's parked outside me own house.

POLICEMAN: Your property only extends as far as those horrible chickens cut out in your hedge.

HANCOCK: Horrible chickens? They are not chickens, mush – *they* are birds of paradise. It's the milkman – his horse has been at 'em. Oh yes – yes, he has the cart up on the pavement getting at those. I shall be glad when he gets electrified and has a cart with a handle to pull round.

POLICEMAN: Be that as it may, your property only extends up to the hedge. The pavement and the roadway thereafter are public thoroughfares, for use without let or hindrance to the public at large. *Move* it.

HANCOCK: I will not 'move it'. There is no law to say a man

may not park his car outside his own front door.

POLICEMAN: Well, normally we don't mind, we don't bother about short periods, but that car hasn't been moved for ten years.

SID: Ten *years*? Do you mean to tell me you've had us cleaning that car every day and you never *use* it?

HANCOCK: Well . . . I . . . I get in the driving seat sometimes, and I turn the wheel, and a bit of 'vroom-vroom, vroom-vroom' . . . and pretend, and that – but if you mean actually moving . . . no.

BILL *(ominously)*: Why not?

HANCOCK: Because I can't pass the test! I've been up seventy-three times, and they keep failing me. I just can't get the hang of it . . . me feet are too big, that's the trouble. They overlap. I put me foot on the brake, half of it goes on the accelerator as well, and we're off again.

POLICEMAN: Your feet are no concern of mine. That car must be moved.

HANCOCK: It's doing no harm, it's only standing there.

POLICEMAN: It *is* doing harm – this road has been resurfaced eight times since the war – all except the bit your car is standing on. Here – I measured it just now. It's eight inches lower than the rest of the road. We want to fill it in, so *move it!*

HANCOCK: I will not move it!

POLICEMAN: Those are your last words?

HANCOCK: They are, sir!

POLICEMAN: Very well. Under the powers now invested in us by the new traffic act, I shall make arrangements for the car to be towed away.

HANCOCK: You will do no such thing! Putting chains onto my front bumper and lifting it up onto its hind legs – they'd scratch it! I've lavished hours of loving care on that car, and I'm not having it desecrated by the likes of you!

POLICEMAN: It's got to be moved!

HANCOCK: It cannot be moved, I have got nowhere to put it!

POLICEMAN: Put it in a garridge!

HANCOCK: I have not got a gar*arge*.

POLICEMAN: Then put it in your front garden. Knock down them chickens and push it through there.

17,000

HANCOCK: That's the trouble with the country today – I

mean, there's no respect for the aristocracy at all. I am *not* moving that car – there it is, and there it stays. Until such time as I have passed my test and can afford a gallon of petrol. I know my rights – this is not a main road, no buses run down here, there are no zebra crossings, it's well away from all corners, and there are two of my own hurricane lamps lighting it up. Taking things all round, therefore, I am perfectly within my rights parking my car there – and I shall resist any efforts to move it.

POLICEMAN: But we've got to mend the road!

HANCOCK: Then you'll just have to mend round it again. And tell the tar-sprayer to watch what he's doing. I had to chisel open the door last time.

POLICEMAN: Yes, but don't you see . . .

HANCOCK: There is no more to be said. 'Might is not right – temper it with justice'. Rex versus Crippen – third day, Crippen speaking, 79 for 3. So if you will kindly take your helmet off the teapot, I shall bid you good day.

POLICEMAN: Very well. I shall have to make a report, and no doubt you will be hearing from the magistrate's court within the next few days.

HANCOCK: Good! And I shall answer any charge in person! I am willing to defend my civil liberties, whatever you try to do to me. I'm not frightened! Use your rubber hoses – and your lights in the face – and all smoking while I haven't got one, see if I care! And it's no good trying to come round to tow it away because I'm taking the wheels off! . . . That showed him. They've met their match in me. Now, let's finish me dinner. I bet he thought . . . Where's me cauliflower cheese gone? Who has had my cauli- . . . it's her, she's woofed it – she's like greased lightning – I only took me eyes off it for thirty seconds. I bet it never touched the sides on its way down. Stone me, no wonder the dustmen don't bother to call here. All they get is ashes. Oh, spread me some bread and dripping.

GRAMS: MUSIC LINK.

JUDGE: Fined twenty-five shillings, licence endorsed. Next case, constable, please.

2ND POLICEMAN: John Dillinger, driving across ploughed field looking for proposed London–Birmingham roadway.

JUDGE: Ah – drunk?

2ND POLICEMAN: Yes.

JUDGE: Five pounds, disqualified six months. Next?

2ND POLICEMAN: Jack Bradley, over ninety miles an hour up the wrong side of a dual carriageway.

JUDGE: Over ninety miles an hour?

2ND POLICEMAN: It must have been – it didn't even make a white blob on our radar screen.

JUDGE: Four pounds, licence endorsed. Next?

2ND POLICEMAN: Anthony Hancock, parking ten years.

HANCOCK: Not guilty, your honour – I wish to defend meself!

JUDGE *(to himself)*: Oh dear, why do they bother? *(To Hancock:)* Must you?

HANCOCK: I must! In the fair name of British Justice and Liberty I demand my rights as a citizen.

JUDGE: Oh dear, he's one of those . . . Very well, continue.

HANCOCK: M'lud, m'lud – my car has been parked outside 23 Railway Cuttings – my own abode, mark you – in a de-restricted street, without any complaints from the neighbours, passing pedestrians or cars. It does no harm, it merely enhances the neighbourhood with its beauty. In my profession it is essential to have a motor vehicle at my disposal all hours of the day, in case I have to dash off to rehearsals.

JUDGE: But you haven't used it for ten years.

HANCOCK: So you can see I am in no position to pay the fine. But I may get some work any day now – and you have to be there quick in case somebody else gets it. Therefore – I submit – that there is no case to answer. *(Lapsing into Q.C. impression.)* I am perfectly within my rights to leave my car where it is! There is no *law* to prevent me doing so . . . there is nothing anyone can do to stop me! And, therefore . . . I demand . . . yes, demand! . . . that I be found not guilty – discharged – and walk from this court a free man!

JUDGE: Fined forty shillings. Next?

HANCOCK: But, m'lud! . . .

JUDGE: Fined forty-five shillings. Next?

HANCOCK: I object, your honour!

JUDGE: *Fifty* shillings – next?

HANCOCK: This is a travesty of justice!

JUDGE: Fifty-five shillings . . . will you allow me to get on with the next case, or will you go on to the three pounds? Oh, and one other thing . . .

HANCOCK: Yes?

JUDGE: Move it! Next?

2ND POLICEMAN: Judge Percy Francis.

JUDGE: That's me!

2ND POLICEMAN: Yes sir – your car is parked outside in a restricted area.

JUDGE: Oh, I see – well, fined fifty – er, *ten* shillings; licence endorsed – I mean, don't do it again – court adjourned, this is ridiculous!

GRAMS: MUSIC LINK.

HANCOCK: I am *not* moving it!

SID: You got to, son – the court ruled against you.

HANCOCK: They have no right to make me move my car. I've got nowhere to put it!

SID: Well, they reckon you could leave it out on the front garden.

HANCOCK: I am not ruining my glads and daffs for anybody. It's taken me three years to get those bulbs right. You wait till they come up. I've got me coat of arms in one bed, and there's the number of the house in another; and then there's me face in the centre.

SID: Very nice . . . I thought you were going to have a clock?

HANCOCK: Well, it's combined. Me face is the dial, and the hands are stuck on me nose. So when they're pointing to each ear it's ten to two.

SID: Oh, I've got it – and at quarter past three you're going to look like Jimmy Edwards.

HANCOCK: That's it. So you see, I can't have me car in the front garden, it'll completely spoil it. And besides, to get it in, I'll have to tear down me chickens . . . me birds of paradise, and I'm not doing that either.

MISS PUGH: Anyone for stuffed cabbage?

HANCOCK *(firmly)*: No.

SID: No.

MISS PUGH: Good, I'll make some. Where's Bill?

HANCOCK: He's outside, cleaning the car. The eleven-twenty-three to Waterloo went by just now. Fifteen direct hits, and two clouds of smoke.

BILL: Tub – come quickly.

HANCOCK: What's wrong?

BILL: The police have arrived with a breakdown waggon – they're going to tow the car away – they're putting the chains round it now.

HANCOCK: You fool! – why didn't you stop them?

BILL: Well, I tried to – they put the hook under me collar and swung me over the fence.

HANCOCK: If you've landed on my flower beds –

BILL: I didn't do much damage, Tub – I missed the chickens, but I think I landed on your snowdrops.

HANCOCK: You nincompoop! Do you realize what this means? When me face grows I won't have any teeth! I shall deal with you later. I'm going to have some words with these blue-coated vandals.

FX: DOOR OPENS.

HANCOCK: Take those chains off my car! I'll have the law on you!

POLICEMAN: We *are* the law. We warned you, you had your chance – you wouldn't move it, so now we're moving it for you. Fred – hitch it up to the lorry.

HANCOCK: Oh no you don't – you're not taking my car away. Bill – lie down in the road in front of the lorry.

BILL: Hey, Tub . . .

HANCOCK: Lie down in front of the lorry!

BILL: But they might run me over!

HANCOCK: This is a chance I'm going to have to take. Lie down.

POLICEMAN: Now come along, sir – don't be foolish. Get up out of the road.

HANCOCK: You stay there, Bill – they can't trample roughshod over private citizens.

POLICEMAN: Are you going to get up, sir?

BILL: No – you're not going to touch my friend's car, so there!

POLICEMAN: Right, Fred – lower the hook! . . . Hook it under his belt . . . haul away . . . That's it, swing him clear . . .

BILL: Put me down!

HANCOCK: Yes, you put my friend down!

POLICEMAN: That's it, Fred, swing him over the hedge . . .

BILL: Help, Tub, help!

HANCOCK: I demand you release him!

POLICEMAN: Right-ho, Fred, let him go!

HANCOCK: Not over me flower-beds! . . . Stone me – that's me nose and one of me ears gone for a burton. You've disfigured my clock, you vandals – I'll sue you for damages!

BILL: I think I've broken some bones, Tub.

HANCOCK: Oh, shut up. I shall write to the vicar about this!

POLICEMAN: Right, Fred – get the hook round the bumper again. That's it . . . right, haul away.

GRAMS: HAULING NOISES.

HANCOCK: Be careful, it won't take the strain!

GRAMS: TWANG, CRASH.

POLICEMAN: Well, that's the bumper moved, anyway. Throw it in the back of the lorry. Fred – drive round and hitch up the other bumper – we'll get it from behind.

HANCOCK: Leave it alone! There'll be questions asked in the House about this!

GRAMS: EXPRESS TRAIN.

HANCOCK: Hullo – the eleven-forty-one to Victoria – duck, everybody, behind the fence!

GRAMS: MUSIC LINK.

SID: Well, you won the first round, Hancock – your car's still there.

HANCOCK: Of course it's still there. They've come up against a fighter in me.

SID: Well, you had a bit of help, boy. You were dead lucky that train went past just then. That copper didn't know what time it was when that lump of coal hit him on the back of the head.

HANCOCK: He still doesn't. He hasn't come round yet. He's in the Cottage Hospital.

SID: Ha ha ha . . . good shots, those train drivers, ain't they? They missed the other one, so I picked up a brick and let him have it. He thinks it was them! Where's Bill?

HANCOCK: Oh, he's still lying out in the flower-bed moaning and groaning.

SID: Don't you think we ought to go out and bring him in?

HANCOCK: No, if he wants to come in, let him crawl in. Great oaf – falling on me set piece. Skylarking about on cranes – it's his own fault.

MISS PUGH: They'll be back, you know. They won't let you get away with it. You can't fight the law. (*Hopefully.*) They'll put you in jail for this!

HANCOCK: You always put the mockers on everything, don't you? Why don't you get back in the kitchen and mind your own business – what is for dinner?

MISS PUGH: You don't like stuffed marrow, do you?

HANCOCK: No I do not.

MISS PUGH: Well that's what we're having, then.

HANCOCK: Stuffed marrow, stuffed cabbage, and cauliflower cheese! Can't you forget you used to work in a British Restaurant? She doesn't half cook some rubbish – all her war-time recipes here – Potato Pete stuck up in the kitchen, there – it's not good enough for a gourmet like me, a man of my taste! The war's over, dear, there's other food about now! I've got a very delicate palate – nothing but the finest – subtle, exotic, fleeting savouries, that's what I want. Why can't we have egg and chips and a bottle of chop sauce? We never get anything imaginative round here.

BILL: Tub – Tub . . .

HANCOCK: Oh, it's you – he can't be too badly hurt, he opened the door by himself. What do you want?

BILL: They're back, Tub – they've got the road-menders ready to start as soon as the car's moved.

HANCOCK: Well they won't move it this time – it's bolted to the road and chained to the lamp-post.

BILL: They're not trying to move it this time – they've got a great big steam-roller up against it – they reckon it'll just about fill in the hole, then all they've got to do is spray some tar over it.

HANCOCK: They can't do that! Bill – go and lay in front of the steam-roller.

BILL: No – I can't do that, Tub, I can't move!

HANCOCK: Sid – help me carry him out there – open the door . . . get his feet . . . to you . . . *(Etc.)*

BILL: Put me down – stop it – I don't want to be flattened! I don't want to be part of the road!

HANCOCK: Not so much of the old lip, there. Hey – keep that steam-roller away from my limousine!

POLICEMAN: Now, we don't want any more trouble, sir. I'm willing to forget the last little frack-ass, but we're not having any more.

HANCOCK: It wasn't my fault – I told you to duck. How's your head?

POLICEMAN: Nasty. Quite nasty. All these bandages – I can't get me helmet on.

HANCOCK: Never mind – paint them all black and stick a badge on them, nobody will notice. Right, Sid – put him down in front of the steam-roller.

POLICEMAN: Now come along – now get up. Laying in front of steam-rollers is forbidden in this country.

BILL: I can't move – me ankle's gone.

POLICEMAN: Look, sir, we can't go on like this, can we?

HANCOCK: No, we can't.

POLICEMAN: This bit of road under your car must be brought up to the same level as the rest of the road, it's dangerous otherwise.

HANCOCK: I appreciate your point, officer, but I am not moving my car. I refuse to be coerced.

POLICEMAN: Well, then, let's talk it over – let's have what we might call a 'summit conference', between the 'heads of state'.

HANCOCK: Well, I'm always open to reason. What are your proposals to end the cold war?

POLICEMAN: Well, how about this – we move your car twenty yards up the road until this bit's levelled up and re-surfaced, then you can move it back and we say no more about it.

HANCOCK: That seems very reasonable. You guarantee that I won't have any more trouble?

POLICEMAN: No – not for another ten years till we have to fill the road in again.

HANCOCK: Very well – I agree.

POLICEMAN: Thank you very much, sir.

HANCOCK: I mean, you'll appreciate . . . I mean, there was nothing personal against your good self. Throughout the whole affair you conducted yourself with the utmost dignity and in a fashion most befitting a member of the Cheam Constabulary.

POLICEMAN: Thank you, sir. I must say I've admired your, er, tenacity in standing up for your rights.

HANCOCK: Thank you.

POLICEMAN: Are we friends again?

HANCOCK: Certainly. Little fingers? Well – old man – help me push the car along and we can start immediately.

POLICEMAN: What about him in the road?

HANCOCK: Oh, push him in the gutter – he'll probably fall asleep.

GRAMS: MUSIC LINK.

SID: Well, congratulations, Hancock – you did it. The car's back in its rightful position. I never thought you'd do it.

HANCOCK: It just shows you that when you believe in something you've got to fight for it.

GRAMS: EXPRESS TRAIN.

SID: Hullo – the ten-forty-two to Waterloo's going by.

HANCOCK: There they go – they've started heaving coal at it

again.

SID: Here – blimey, they're hitting it every time – look!

HANCOCK: They'll smash it up – great chunks going through the windows – look, me windscreen's gone! Look – four bits gone through the hood!

SID: Their aim's improving, in'nit! They haven't missed once – they must have a rangefinder on board. Here, Hancock, that car won't be able to take much more punishment like that – I can't understand it – they've never been so accurate before.

HANCOCK: Well of course – I've just realized – you know what's happened – their aim hasn't improved at all. Now the road's been built up the car's up much higher – they can see it better. They've got more to aim at. I knew I should have held out and not let them do that road.

SID: Well, what are you going to do about it then, move the car?

HANCOCK: No I am not. There is only one way to deal with this – we've got to stop those trains going by. Bill . . .

BILL: Yeah?

HANCOCK: Come here.

BILL: What do you want?

HANCOCK: Go and lay on the railway line.

BILL: No I won't!

HANCOCK: Grab him . . . Miss Pugh, some rope – we'll tie him across the line.

BILL: No, Tub, please – don't do it.

HANCOCK: Take his legs, we've got to stop the twelve-twenty-three.

BILL: Why am I always the one . . .

HANCOCK: Look it won't hurt, Bill, you just lay in front of the train – we'll see who gives in first.

BILL: Yes, but I always get the . . .

HANCOCK: You can trust me, Bill – we're not going to take this lying down – well, I mean, you are, but . . .

BILL: Oh, no, not this time . . .

HANCOCK: It's the only way – force must match force . . . *(Argument fades under:)*

GRAMS: SIGNATURE TUNE.

ANNOUNCER: That was Hancock's Half-Hour, starring Tony Hancock, with Sidney James, Bill Kerr, Hattie Jacques and Kenneth Williams. Theme and incidental music composed and conducted by Wally Stott; the show written by Alan Simpson and Ray Galton. The programme, which was recorded, was produced by Tom Ronald.

'THE HITCH-HIKER'S GUIDE TO THE GALAXY'

The Hitch-Hiker's Guide to the Galaxy, that useful book with the words 'DON'T PANIC' in large friendly letters on the front, has this to say about Douglas Adams:

Douglas Adams was born on a small world in the unfashionable end of the Western Spiral Arm of the Galaxy, and was what the ape-descendants of that world like to regard as 'educated' at Cambridge University; from where he went on to write the alarmingly popular saga of Arthur Dent, and his friend Ford Prefect who turned out to come from Betelgeuse and not from Guildford after all. Starting life as a radio serial, this story has subsequently become a gramophone record, a television serial, three books, a video disc, a Galaxy-distributed stereo-feelie directed by Francis Ford Coppola VI, and was finally digitally encoded onto the contents of seventeen tins of Gruyère cheese.

This extract from the second episode of the original radio series begins after Ford and Arthur have been rescued from certain death after being ejected from a Vogon spaceship.

THE BOOK ....Peter Jones
ARTHUR DENT ....Simon Jones
FORD PREFECT ....Geoffrey McGivern
ZAPHOD BEEBLEBROX ....Mark Wing-Davey
TRILLIAN ....Susan Sheridan
and
MARVIN, *the paranoid android* ...Stephen Moore

The episode first broadcast on 15 March 1978.

ZAPHOD: Who are they, Trillian?

TRILLIAN: Oh, just a couple of guys we picked up in open space – Sector ZZ9, plural Z Alpha.

ZAPHOD: Yes, yes – well, that's a very sweet thought, Trillian, but do you think it's really *wise* under the circumstances – I mean, here we are, on the run and everything, we've got the police of half the galaxy after us and we stop to pick up hitch-hikers – OK, so, ten out of ten for style, but minus several million for good thinking, OK?

TRILLIAN: Zaphod – they were floating unprotected in open space – you didn't want them to die, did you?

ZAPHOD: Well, not as such, no, but—

TRILLIAN: Anyway, I didn't pick them up – the ship did it all by itself, whilst we were in improbability drive.

ZAPHOD: That's incredible.

TRILLIAN: No, just very very improbable. Look – don't worry about the aliens – they're just a couple of guys, I expect. I'll send the robot down to check them out. Hey, Marvin.

(Sound of robot approaching.)

MARVIN: I THINK YOU OUGHT TO KNOW I'M FEELING VERY DEPRESSED.

ZAPHOD: God!

TRILLIAN: Well, here's something to occupy you and keep your mind off things.

MARVIN: IT WON'T WORK. I HAVE AN EXCEPTIONALLY LARGE MIND.

TRILLIAN: Marvin. . . .

MARVIN: ALL RIGHT, WHAT DO YOU WANT ME TO DO?

TRILLIAN: Go down to number two entry bay and bring the two aliens up here under surveillance.

MARVIN: JUST THAT?

TRILLIAN: Yes.

MARVIN: I WON'T ENJOY IT.

ZAPHOD: She's not asking you to enjoy it – just *do* it, will you?

MARVIN: ALL RIGHT, I'LL DO IT.

ZAPHOD: Good, great – thank you.

MARVIN: I'M NOT GETTING YOU DOWN AT ALL, AM I?

TRILLIAN: No, no, Marvin, that's just fine, really.

MARVIN: I WOULDN'T LIKE TO THINK I WAS GETTING YOU DOWN.

TRILLIAN: No – don't worry about that, you just act as comes naturally, and everything will be fine.

MARVIN: YOU'RE SURE YOU DON'T MIND?

ZAPHOD: *No*, no, it's all just part of life.

MARVIN: LIFE – DON'T TALK TO ME ABOUT LIFE. *(Exits.)*

TRILLIAN: I don't think I can stand that robot much longer, Zaphod.

THE BOOK: *The* Encyclopaedia Galactica *defines a robot as a mechanical apparatus designed to do the work of a man. The Marketing Division of the Sirius Cybernetics Corporation defines a robot as 'Your plastic pal who's fun to be with'. The* Hitch-Hiker's Guide to the Galaxy *defines the Marketing Division of the Sirius Cybernetics Corporation as 'a bunch of mindless jerks who will be the first against the wall when the revolution comes', with a footnote to the effect that the editors would welcome applications from anyone interested in taking over the post of robotics correspondent. Curiously enough, an edition of the* Encyclopaedia Galactica *that fell through a time-warp from a thousand years in the future defined the Marketing Division of the Sirius Cybernetics Corporation as 'a bunch of mindless jerks who were the first against the wall when the revolution came'.*

FORD: I think this ship is brand new, Arthur.

ARTHUR: How can you tell – have you got some exotic device for measuring the age of metal?

FORD: No, I just found this sales brochure lying on the floor. 'The universe can be yours' – and look, I was right – 'Sensational breakthrough in Improbability physics – as the ship's drive reaches infinite improbability, it passes through every conceivable point in every conceivable universe almost simultaneously. You select your own re-entry point. Be the envy of other major governments.' This is big league stuff.

ARTHUR: It looks a hell of a lot better than that dingy Vogon ship. This is my idea of a space ship. All gleaming white, flashing lights, everything. What happens if I press this button?

FORD *(hurriedly)*: I wouldn't.

FX: BEEP.

ARTHUR: Oh . . .

FORD: What happened?

ARTHUR: A sign lit up, saying 'Please do not press this button again'.

FORD: They make a big thing of the ship's cybernetics. 'A new generation of Sirius Cybernetics Corporation robots and computers, with the new GPP feature.'

ARTHUR: GPP – what's that?

FORD: Er – it says 'Genuine People Personalities'.

ARTHUR: Sounds ghastly.

(Door opens.)

DOOR *(contentedly)*: Ahhhh!

(Enter Marvin.)

MARVIN: IT IS.

ARTHUR: What?

MARVIN: GHASTLY. IT ALL IS. ABSOLUTELY GHASTLY. JUST DON'T EVEN TALK ABOUT IT. LOOK AT THIS DOOR – 'ALL THE DOORS IN THIS SPACECRAFT HAVE A CHEERFUL AND SUNNY DISPOSITION. IT IS THEIR PLEASURE TO OPEN FOR YOU, AND THEIR SATISFACTION TO CLOSE AGAIN WITH THE KNOWLEDGE OF A JOB WELL DONE.'

DOOR: Mmmmmmm – yummmm. *(Closes.)*

MARVIN: HATEFUL, ISN'T IT? COME ON – I'VE BEEN ORDERED TO TAKE YOU UP TO THE BRIDGE. HERE I AM, BRAIN THE SIZE OF A PLANET AND THEY TELL ME TO TAKE YOU UP TO THE BRIDGE. CALL THAT JOB SATISFACTION, 'COS I DON'T.

FORD: Excuse me – which Government owns this ship?

MARVIN: YOU WATCH THIS DOOR. IT'S ABOUT TO OPEN AGAIN. I CAN TELL BY THE INTOLERABLE AIR OF SMUGNESS IT SUDDENLY GENERATES. COME ON.

DOOR *(opening)*: Glad to be of service. Mmmmmm.

MARVIN: THANK YOU THE MARKETING DIVISION OF THE SIRIUS CYBERNETICS CORPORATION.

DOOR: You're welcome. Mmmmmm. *(Closes.)*

MARVIN: 'LET'S BUILD ROBOTS WITH GENUINE PEOPLE PERSONALITIES', THEY SAID. SO THEY TRIED IT OUT WITH ME. I'M A PERSONALITY PROTOTYPE. YOU CAN TELL, CAN'T YOU?

FORD: Ummm . . .

MARVIN: I HATE THAT DOOR. I'M NOT GETTING YOU DOWN, AM I?

FORD: Which Government owns this ship?

MARVIN: *NO* GOVERNMENT OWNS IT. IT'S BEEN STOLEN.

FORD & ARTHUR: Stolen!?

MARVIN: STOLEN.

FORD: Who by?

MARVIN: ZAPHOD BEEBLEBROX.

FORD: *Zaphod Beeblebrox?*

MARVIN: SORRY, DID I SAY SOMETHING WRONG? PARDON ME FOR BREATHING WHICH I NEVER DO ANYWAY, SO I DON'T KNOW WHY I BOTHER TO SAY IT. OH GOD, I'M SO DEPRESSED. HERE'S ANOTHER OF THOSE SELF-SATISFIED DOORS. LIFE – DON'T TALK TO ME ABOUT LIFE.

DOOR: Mmmmm – yummmmm.

ARTHUR: No-one even mentioned it!

* * *

MARVIN: . . . AND THEN OF COURSE I'VE GOT THIS TERRIBLE PAIN IN ALL THE DIODES DOWN MY LEFT SIDE.

ARTHUR *(grimly)*: Is that so?

MARVIN: OH YES – I MEAN, I'VE ASKED FOR THEM TO BE REPLACED, BUT NO-ONE EVER LISTENS.

ARTHUR: I can imagine.

TRILLIAN *(watching them on a monitor)*: Oh, God – I don't believe it!

FORD: Well well well . . . Zaphod Beeblebrox.

ZAPHOD: I don't believe it – this is just *too* amazing. Look Trillian, I'll just handle this . . . is anything wrong?

TRILLIAN: I think I'll just wait in the cabin. I'll be back in a minute.

ZAPHOD: Oh, this is going to be great! I'm going to be so unbelievably cool about it, it would flummox a Vegan snow-lizard. This is *terrific*! What real cool – several million points out of ten for style.

TRILLIAN: Well, you enjoy yourself, Zaphod. I don't see what's so great, myself. I'll go and listen for the police on the sub-ether waveband. *(Exits.)*

ZAPHOD: Right . . . which is *the* most nonchalant chair to be discovered working at? . . . Yeah . . . OK . . .

DOOR *(opening)*: Glad to be of service. Mmmmmm. *(Enter Marvin, Ford and Arthur.)*

MARVIN: I SUPPOSE YOU'LL WANT TO SEE THE ALIENS NOW. DO YOU WANT ME TO SIT IN A CORNER AND RUST, OR JUST FALL APART WHERE I'M STANDING?

JONATHAN MILLER

Miller had just qualified as a doctor when he was asked to join Peter Cook, Alan Bennett and Dudley Moore in writing and performing *Beyond the Fringe* in 1960. He always intended to go back into medicine, regarding performing as something of an intrusion in his career; indeed his agonizing over his feelings that he ought to be concentrating on being a doctor when *Beyond the Fringe* was running in New York led Peter Cook to announce that *he* wanted to be a nun. Miller turned from writing and performing to theatre directing shortly afterwards, so that comic pieces by him are a relative rarity. This monologue, which appeared in *Beyond the Fringe*, goes back even further – Miller performed a version of it in BBC radio's *Saturday Night on the Light* (i.e. Light Programme) on 11 January 1958.

'The Heat-Death of the Universe'

Some years ago, when I was rather hard up, I wanted to buy myself a new pair of trousers – but being hard up, I could not afford to buy a new pair. However, some kind friend told me that if I looked sharp about it I could get myself a very nice second-hand pair from the Sales Department of the London Passenger Transport Board Lost Property. Now before I accepted this interesting offer I got involved in a certain amount of fastidious conflict with my inner soul as I was not very keen to assume the trousers which some lunatic had taken off on a train going eastbound towards Whitechapel.

However, after a certain amount of moral contortion in this area, I managed to steel myself to the alien crutch, and made my way towards the shop in question, praying as I did so, 'Oh, God, let them be dry-cleaned when I get there.' And when I arrived there, you can imagine my pleasure and surprise when I found, instead of a dishevelled heap of lunatics' trousers lying all over the place, a very neat heap of brand-new, bright blue corduroy trousers. There were four hundred of them. How can anyone lose four hundred pairs of trousers on a train? I mean, it's hard enough to lose a brown paper bag full of old orange peel when you really try very hard. Besides which, four hundred men wearing no trousers in the rush hour— No, it's obviously part of a London Passenger Transport Board plot – a rather complex economic scheme along Galbraithian or Keynesian lines – something rather baroque to expand the economy. So we go over to investigate this to the London Passenger Transport Board Economics Planning Division Ops Room:

'Carry on Smoking. Operation Cerulean Trousers. Now we are going to issue each one of you men a brand-new, bright blue pair of corduroy trousers. Your job will be to spread out to all parts of London, to empty railway carriages, and there in the darkness and solitude you are to divest yourselves of these garments and leave them in horrid little heaps on the floors of the carriages concerned. Do I make myself absolutely clear? Good – well, on your way. Godspeed, chins up and trousers down!'

Then out into the blue of the night the four hundred men disperse identically in blue corduroy trousers, trying to look as inconspicuous as a great massed phalanx of four hundred men dressed in identical blue corduroy trousers possibly can look. And they disperse to places far out on the ends of the Central Line, places out on the Essex marshes, which are totally uninhabited, one presumes, except for a few stray wading marsh birds mournfully pacing the primeval slime.

And there in the moonlit sidings they let themselves separately and individually into the empty compartments and just before the final awful existential act of detrouserment they do some of those things people sometimes do in railway compartments when they think they are alone . . . or, indeed, alone anywhere for that matter. Things like . . . well, things like smelling their own armpits.

Of course, it's quite possible the men did not remove their trousers in the compartments at all but with a proper sense of privacy made their way along the corridor to the locked seclusion of the lavatory. Now English Railway lavatories have a rather mysterious, unpunctuated motto printed on the wall, saying 'Gentlemen lift the seat.' Now, what exactly does this mean? It could be a blunt military order – it might be an invitation to upper-class larceny—

Anyway, one way or the other, off come the trousers and then the four hundred half-naked men make their way back to headquarters through the sleeping chilly streets of nocturnal London – four hundred fleet white nude figures in the night, their eight hundred horny feet pattering on the pavements and arousing small children from their slumbers in upstairs bedrooms. Children who are soothed back into their sleep by their parents with the ancient words, 'Turn your face to the wall, my darling, while the gentlemen trot by.'

‘ROUND THE HORNE’

In his radio series *Much-Binding-in-the-Marsh* and *Beyond Our Ken*, as well as *Round The Horne*, Kenneth Horne was the calm centre round which an extraordinary collection of characters revolved – none more extraordinary than the pair of outrageous queers, Julian and Sandy, played respectively by Hugh Paddick and Kenneth Williams. This example comes from the broadcast of 28 April 1968. The sketch was written by Barry Took.

‘Julian and Sandy – Bona Political Party’

HORNE: Now, Elections are cropping up all the time, but one that escaped notice was in my area. The usual parties were represented – Labour, Conservative and Liberal – but there was one party I'd never heard of before. And the slogan on their posters read, 'Keep Britain Bona.' I decided to find out more about them, so I popped down to their party headquarters.

FX: DOOR OPENS.

HORNE: Hello – anybody there?

JULIAN: Oh, hello – I'm Julian, and this is my friend Sandy.

SANDY: Oh, hello, Mr. Horne . . . We are the Universal Party – so called because we're at it right, left and centre . . . Shake hands with your prospective member.

JULIAN: That's me, Mr. Horne.

HORNE: You, Julian?

JULIAN: Yes, I stand behind the working man . . .

SANDY: And I stand behind Julie – I'm his campaign manager.

JULIAN: He's an old campaigner, Mr. Horne.

SANDY: He don't tell no lies.

HORNE: Now, why have you formed your own party?

SANDY: That's a good question.

JULIAN: Well, we couldn't see eye to eye with the other major parties – we left the Labour Party because we disagreed with the prescription charges . . .

SANDY: And we fell out with the Conservatives because blue isn't our colour!

JULIAN: Makes me right washed out!

SANDY: Makes him looked washed out, it does. Yes, we didn't like the colour of their favours, so, then we was Liberal with our favours . . . for a while . . .

JULIAN: For a while . . .

SANDY: . . . then we felt personally *betrayed* by the action of our Liberal member.

HORNE: Oh – what did he do?

JULIAN: Oh, I can't bring myself to say it, Mr. Horne . . . He . . . (shall I tell him?) . . . He went and got married!

SANDY: Don't carry on, Jules.

JULIAN: Well, I can't help it.

SANDY: Jules – pull yourself together! It's to no avail! Pull yourself together . . . what's done is done! Now blow your nose on your rosette . . .

JULIAN: Then we thought, they've all let us down, so it's time for a change.

SANDY: So we changed.

JULIAN: Yes – we formed our own party.

HORNE: And what's your policy?

JULIAN: Well, we have a three-pronged manifesto.

SANDY: Three distinct prongs, it's got. Yes. Show him, Jule – get out your manifesto.

JULIAN: Oh, yes – well, our points are these – one: double the building programme so there's latties for all . . .

SANDY: Latties for all!

JULIAN: Latties for all.

SANDY: Lovely! Remove the American missiles from our shores . . .

JULIAN: Oh yes! Particularly that one – what's it called, now . . . Polarie, that's it . . .

SANDY: That Polarie, yes . . .

JULIAN: Our third prong – free crow's-feet cream for all! Irrespective of race, creed or sex.

SANDY: Yes – that's your incentive bona.

HORNE: And what about old age pensions?

SANDY: Don't you worry, Mr. Horne, duck, we'll see you all right.

JULIAN: Make special provision for the over-sixties.

SANDY: The smaller sizes won't be left out, neither.

JULIAN: No. I think I can confidently say that I expect a huge poll.

SANDY: Mmm, his name's Vladimir, always comes round . . . pops round of a Wednesday evening, he does.

JULIAN: Old friend of Gordon's.

SANDY: Gordon, yes, Gordon's his friend too . . . here, Jule – got your election address?

JULIAN: Yes, care of the Marine Commando Club, Paddington.

SANDY: No . . . no, not that, you silly prospective member – your speech! Yes, your Polarie, with which you're going to sweep the hustings . . . I can't bear an unswept husting. Go on, Jule, get on your box – not that one, dear, your soap-box!

JULIAN: I don't like to.

SANDY: Go on, – he's shy with crowds, Mr. Horne . . . go on, imagine you're in front of a great ignorant rabble!

JULIAN: Shall I?

SANDY: Mmm, be good practice for you when you go on the Simon Dee show. Now, you heckle him if you want to, Mr. Horne.

HORNE: Right.

SANDY: There – ready, Jule? Mr. Horne – you're about to hear his maiden speech. Go on, love. Go on.

JULIAN: Omies and palones of this borough . . .

SANDY: That's lovely . . .

JULIAN: . . . We are poised at a moment in history. The future could be naff . . .

SANDY: Naff!

JULIAN: . . . Or it could be bona . . .

SANDY: Bona!

JULIAN: The time has come for a frank and honest varda at our awkward position . . .

SANDY: Oh, yes, that's true . . .

JULIAN: I am questing after this seat! . . . For the good of my fellow omies!

SANDY: Yes . . .

JULIAN: Let us not mince . . .

SANDY: Have you taken leave of your senses?

JULIAN: I haven't finished! . . . Let us not mince words!

SANDY: Oh!

JULIAN: Let us put our best lallie forward! . . . and with our eeks shining with hope troll together towards a fantabulosa futurette!

SANDY: Bravo, Jules! I'm right behind you! We'll go all the way with Jules!

HORNE: Well, if you are, would you drop me at Wimbledon Common? I can get a bus from there . . .

SANDY: And now – let us raise our voices, and sing the Party Song.

(Sings:)* 'The Party's flag is deepest puce
With fleur-de-lys in pale chartreuse.

JULIAN: Both working om and nouveau-riche
Will find our programme very chich!

SANDY: We'll do our best for one and old

JULIAN: Our party line is very bold.

* Tune: 'The Red Flag'.

BOTH: Let's mince together in hand
We'll make Great Britain Fairy-Land.'

HORNE: And he didn't get in. Apparently it wasn't a safe seat.

'RUTLAND WEEKEND TELEVISION'

Following his television work with the *Monty Python* team, Eric Idle went on to his own series, made on a shoestring for BBC-2. He continues the typically Python technique of taking a familiar format, emptying the content out of it, and replacing it with something entirely unsuitable – in one sketch he even removes the content from a typical television interview and replaces it with gibberish. In this instance, the format is that of the Stanley Holloway monologues; but the content is entirely Idle's. The show was first broadcast on 17 December 1976.

'Wife-swopping Party Song'

I went to a wife-swapping party
And nobody asked me to swap.
Deirdre, my wife,
Had the time of her life
With the man from the Off-Licence shop.

But *his* wife was minding the business
And he'd only come with the wine,
Still he went round all night,
Swapping on sight,
I do wish he hadn't swapped mine.

Now Deirdre, my wife, she's a shy girl,
And she doesn't like to say 'no'.
And though in her past,
She's never been fast,
Last night she never went slow.

But I sat all night at the orgy,
And no one asked me to indulge.
The things that I saw,
Going on on the floor,
Would make your eyes goggle and bulge.

There were things that they did to each other,
In places I've not seen before,
They were at it like knives
With each other's wives.
By golly I bet they'll be sore.

Finally my flabber was gasted
When our grocer, I know him on sight
Took a — and put it in someone's —
With a — by the — near the light.
Then they all kind of — and then tickled
With a —, it was really obscene.
I've never seen it attempted;
I do hope their underwear's clean.

My night at the wife-swapping party
Has certainly shattered a dream,
Our hostess they said was
Tucked up in bed
With half of the Sunderland Team.

But her husband, our host, he's a nice chap,
He said as he gave me my coat,
'Odd man out I can see',
Put his hand on my knee,
And then stuck his tongue down my throat.

Well, I'm not a chap who is prudish
I don't mind a wee bit of fun,
But I do draw the line at perversion
There are some things that shouldn't be done.
In fact, if I'm honest, we did them
Twice, or three times, maybe four,
Right there and then
With a bent friend called Ben
On the rug on the living room floor.

Well 'chaque à son gout' is my motto
And we 'chaque'd à son gout' all night long,
Till mid-way through the strife
I met Deirdre, my wife,
With the grocer and his — going strong.

'What on earth are you doing,' she said, 'Gerald?'
'I don't rightly know,' I replied.
'It's something in Latin'
And she without battin'
An eyelid said, 'Come on outside.'

My god there was a heck of a hoo-ha
About who had done what with who's heck
And Deirdre said she was just tasting wine
Just tasting wine? Bloody neck!
She had more in her hand than a bottle . . .
Still, it's all turned out quite all right,
'Cos we decided we both loved each other.
(Pause.) And we're going again tonight.

'YES MINISTER'

Easily the wittiest and best written of recent television comedy, *Yes Minister* combines the comedy experience and political observation of both Jonathan Lynn and Antony Jay to produce a picture of Whitehall at work which carries an alarming ring of authenticity – it is allegedly Mrs. Thatcher's favourite programme. This episode, from the third series, is unusual in taking its protagonists – Jim Hacker, the Minister for Administrative Affairs; Permanent Under-Secretary Sir Humphrey Appleby; and Private Secretary Bernard Woolley – on a foreign diplomatic mission.

JIM HACKER, M.P. ....Paul Eddington
SIR HUMPHREY APPLEBY ......Nigel Hawthorne
BERNARD WOOLLEY ....Derek Fowlds
ANNIE HACKER ....Diana Hoddinott
BILL PRITCHARD ....Antony Carrick
JENNY GOODWIN ....April Walker
FIRST ARAB ....Vic Tablian
SECOND ARAB ....Sam Dastor
PRINCE MOHAMMED ....Walter Randall
ROSS ....Michael Sharvell-Martin

Script by Antony Jay and Jonathan Lynn
First broadcast 2 December 1982 on BBC-2

'The Moral Dimension'

Interior of an aircraft. Jim and Humphrey are walking down the aisle and taking their seats. Annie and Bernard sit down behind them.

JIM: You're sure we can't be accused of wasting lots of Government money on this trip?

HUMPHREY: Absolutely, Minister.

JIM: And we *are* taking the smallest possible delegation?

HUMPHREY: Absolutely. Pared to the bone.

JIM *(looking out of window)*: Who are all those people? *(We see a line of forty or fifty officials with Government briefcases getting onto the plane.)*

HUMPHREY: Our little delegation.

JIM: You said it had been pared to the bone.

HUMPHREY: So it has.

JIM: Who are they?

HUMPHREY: Well, to start with, a small delegation from the Foreign and Commonwealth Office . . .

JIM: But this is a D.A.A. mission.

HUMPHREY: Yes, well we *are* going abroad. Foreign policy is at stake. We are going to ratify a contract for one of the biggest export orders Britain has ever obtained in the Persian Gulf.

JIM: But that was all negotiated by British Electronic Systems Limited. What do we need with all these Civil Servants? Who are all the rest?

HUMPHREY: Well, there's a delegation from the Department of Trade, and one from Industry. There's a small group from Energy – after all, we are going to an oil Sheikdom. There's a Deputy Secretary leading a team from the Cabinet Office; there's the group from the Central Office of Information; then there's our own team from the D.A.A. . . . *(Shot of the line of officials.)* Press Secretaries, Private Secretaries, liaison with other departments, secretaries, those from the legal department who did the contract, those who supervised the contract . . .

JIM: Pared to the bone?

HUMPHREY *(sadly)*: Pared to the bone. *(He opens his brief-*

case.)

JIM: But when we were going to meet the Kumranis in Middlesborough we were only going to take seven people with us.

HUMPHREY: Well, Teeside is perhaps not quite so diplomatically significant as Kumran.

JIM: Teeside returns four M.Ps.

HUMPHREY: Kumran controls Shell and B.P.

JIM: And what are *you* doing here?

HUMPHREY: Purely my sense of duty-free.

JIM: Duty-free?

HUMPHREY: Duty, free from any personal considerations. Now, perhaps you'd care to look through this, Minister?

JIM: What is it?

HUMPHREY: It's the final communiqué.

JIM: The final communiqué? You can't write the communiqué before you've had the meeting!

HUMPHREY: On the contrary, Minister – you can't write the communiqué *after* you've had the meeting. No, we had to get agreement from half a dozen other departments, from the E.E.C., from Washington, from the Kumrani Embassy – you can't do all that in a few hours in the middle of the desert.

JIM *(reading it)*: But this may bear no relation to what we actually say.

HUMPHREY: No communiqué ever bears any relation to what you actually say.

JIM: Then why have one?

HUMPHREY: Well, it's a sort of exit visa – gets you past the Press Corps. The journalists need it to justify their huge expenses for a futile non-event.

JIM: Non-event!

HUMPHREY: Oh well, of course a brilliant triumph for you, Minister. Which is why it's a futile non-event for the Press.

JIM: I suppose what they'd really like is for me to get drunk at the reception or something.

HUMPHREY *(glumly)*: Not much hope of that. Kumran is dry.

JIM: Well of course it is in the middle of the desert . . . *(Realizes.)* You mean – Islamic Law?

HUMPHREY: Alas, yes.

JIM: We shall be able to get a drink at the British Embassy, shan't we?

HUMPHREY: At the Embassy, yes. But the reception and the dinner are at the Palace. Five hours of orange juice.

JIM: Five hours? Without a single drinkie? Why did you let me come on this trip, Humphrey? What are we going to do? Hip flasks?

HUMPHREY: No, no – much too risky. We have to grin and bear it.

JIM: Why don't we set up a Security Communications Room next door to the reception? You know, emergency telephones, telex lines to Downing Street, all that sort of thing. Then we could fill it with cases of booze brought in from the Embassy.

HUMPHREY: Minister!

JIM: Liven up the orange juice.

HUMPHREY: That is a stroke of genius!

JIM: Can it be done?

HUMPHREY: Well, a Special Communications Room would need a major crisis . . .

JIM: Five hours on orange juice *is* a major crisis.

HUMPHREY: Well, the pound *is* under pressure . . .

JIM: Could you arrange it, Humphrey?

HUMPHREY: Well, if those are your instructions, Minister, I think I can guarantee enthusiastic support.

(Cut to a large Arabic palatial reception room. A small room off it has been turned into a temporary 'Communications Room'. There is a large crowd of guests – all with soft drinks, of course. The Arabs in their traditional dress; the British in theirs. Annie and Jim are talking to the First Arab; Annie is holding an early Islamic rosewater jar.)

JIM: It really was awfully generous of you to present me with this really splendid gift.

FIRST ARAB: It is a great pleasure to be able to commemorate this day.

ANNIE: It's so beautiful.

FIRST ARAB: A magnificent example of seventeenth-century Islamic art.

ANNIE: What was it originally?

FIRST ARAB: A rosewater jar.

JIM: I see . . . for . . . er . . . rosewater, presumably.

FIRST ARAB: Quite so.

BERNARD *(joining them)*: Excuse me, Minister, there is an urgent call for you in the Communications Room. A Mr. Haig.

JIM *(puzzled)*: General Haig?

BERNARD: No, *Mr.* Haig – you know, with the dimples.

JIM *(to First Arab)*: Will you excuse me – most important.

(Jim makes his way to the Communications Room, in which are several phones, a telex, a cypher machine, etc., and a couple of men.)

JIM: I believe there's a message for me from 'Mr. Haig'.

MAN: Yes Minister. *(He takes a bottle of whisky from a red box and puts some into Jim's orange juice.)*

(In the reception hall, Annie and Bernard are now alone, except for a Second Arab who is standing nearby, smiling at them when they look in his direction.)

ANNIE: I'm the only woman here.

BERNARD: Yes, special dispensation. They've made you an Honorary Man for the evening.

ANNIE: This is going to look wonderful on the corner table in our hall.

BERNARD: Oh, well, actually Mrs. Hacker, I'm not sure if . . .

ANNIE: If what?

BERNARD: Well, you see, it's a gift to the Minister.

ANNIE: Well, it's his hall too.

BERNARD: No, what I mean is, I don't think you'll be allowed to keep it.

ANNIE: Why ever not?

BERNARD: Well, I suppose it could be thought, if it *were* valuable it could influence some ministers, I mean not your minister, that is my minister, *our* minister, er, your husband, as it were – as it *is* in fact – I mean, *he* is – I mean – well, *some* ministers . . .

ANNIE: Bernard!

BERNARD: Sorry.

ANNIE: Are you telling me we have to give it back?

BERNARD: Oh, no, no – that would be an insult.

ANNIE: We can't keep it – we can't give it back – what do I do?

BERNARD: Well, it becomes the property of the Government and it's put in a basement somewhere in Whitehall.

ANNIE: Are you *sure* we can't keep it?

BERNARD: Not if it's worth more than about fifty pounds.

ANNIE: How do you find out?

BERNARD: You get a valuation.

ANNIE: Could *you* get a valuation?

BERNARD: Well . . .

ANNIE: Wouldn't it be wonderful if it was less than fifty pounds, because it's awfully pretty.

BERNARD: Well . . . I suppose I could try.

ANNIE: Oh, Bernard, you are wonderful – I don't know what we'd do without you.

(Jim returns with a full glass.)

JIM: Ah, Bernard. You're wanted in the Communications Room. *(Glancing at Second Arab.)* A Mr. John Walker.

BERNARD: Johnny Walker?

JIM: Yes, From the Scotch Office. . . . Scottish Office.

ANNIE: Isn't there a message for me, darling?

JIM: Yes of course there is. Bernard'll get it for you, if you give him your glass . . . *(Glancing at the Arab.)* . . . if you give him your glass, he'll get you some more orange juice, as well. Oh, Bernard – is Humphrey here yet?

BERNARD: Yes, he's just over here, Minister. *(He leads Jim across to where three Arabs in full robes and head-dress are talking with their backs to Bernard and Jim.)* Er, excuse me . . .

(One of the Arabs turns round – it is Humphrey! The second is Ross, from the F.C.O. The third is a real Arab, Prince Mohammed. Bernard disappears to the Communications Room.)

JIM: Humphrey! What on earth? . . .

(Humphrey looks puzzled. Jim indicates his robes.)

HUMPHREY: Traditional Foreign Office courtesy to our Arab hosts – isn't that right, Effendi?

ROSS: Spot on, Humpy. Isn't that right, Your Royal Highness.

PRINCE MOHAMMED: Yes, we regard it as a most warm and gracious compliment.

HUMPHREY: May I present our Minister? Mr. Hacker – this is Prince Mohammed.

JIM: How do you do, Your Royal Highness.

PRINCE MOHAMMED: Pleased to meet you, Your Excellency.

JIM *(pleased)*: Excellency – hmmm! If you will excuse me, I just must have a quick word with Sir Humphrey. *(Takes Humphrey on one side.)* I can't believe my eyes. What are you here as, Ali Baba?

HUMPHREY: Minister, when in Rome . . .

JIM: We are not in Rome, Humphrey. You look ridiculous. I suppose if we were in the Fiji Islands, you'd be dressed in a grass skirt!

HUMPHREY: The Foreign Office takes the view that, as the Arab nations are a very sensitive people, we should show them whose side we're on.

JIM: It may come as a surprise to the Foreign Office, but you're supposed to be on *our* side.

(Ross and Prince Mohammed rejoin them; Bernard re-appears from the Communications Room.)

JIM: Ah, Bernard – any . . . messages in the Communications Room?

BERNARD: There is one for Sir Humphrey, Minister.

HUMPHREY: Oh, good.

BERNARD: The Soviet Embassy is on the line, Sir Humphrey – a Mr. Smirnoff. *(Humphrey goes.)*

JIM: Are you sure there isn't one for me?

BERNARD: Well, there was a message from the British Embassy Compound. The school. A delegation of Teachers.

JIM: Ah. I must go and greet the Teachers. Before the Bell's goes . . . er, the bell goes. *(Exit.)*

PRINCE MOHAMMED: You are receiving a great many very urgent messages.

BERNARD: Yes, yes, we are, aren't we . . .

ROSS: Bernard, excuse me . . . Your Royal Highness, I wonder if I could present Mr. Pennington.

PRINCE MOHAMMED: Excuse me.

BERNARD *(with relief)*: Oh yes, of course, Your Highness.

(Ross and Prince Mohammed go off. Bernard is approached by the Second Arab.)

SECOND ARAB: Excuse me, Effendi, but I could not help overhearing your conversation about valuing the gift. Perhaps I can help.

BERNARD: Oh well, that would be . . . do you have any idea how much?

SECOND ARAB: Of course. An original seventeenth-century rosewater jar is very valuable.

BERNARD: Oh dear.

SECOND ARAB: You are not pleased?

BERNARD: Yes . . . and no. You see, if it is too valuable, the Minister won't be allowed to keep it, and I was rather hoping it wasn't.

SECOND ARAB *(understanding immediately)*: Ah. Well, as I was saying, an original seventeenth-century rosewater jar is very valuable, but this copy, though excellently done, is not of the same order.

BERNARD: Oh, good. About how much?

SECOND ARAB: I would be interested to hear *your* guess.

BERNARD: Oh . . . well, a little under fifty pounds?

SECOND ARAB: Brilliant. Quite a connoisseur.

BERNARD: And you would sign a valuation certificate?

SECOND ARAB: But of course. Your English customs are very strange.

BERNARD: Oh? Why?

SECOND ARAB: You are so strict about a little gift. And yet your Electronics company pays our Finance Minister a million dollars for his co-operation in securing this contract. Is this not strange?

BERNARD *(horrified)*: You don't mean . . .

SECOND ARAB: Of course. I work for the Finance Ministry. I got my share of the money.

BERNARD: For what?

SECOND ARAB: For keeping my mouth shut.

BERNARD: I see. Would you excuse me for a moment? *(Crosses to Jim and Humphrey; agitated and urgent.)* Minister, could I have a private word with Sir Humphrey?

JIM: You may speak freely, Bernard.

BERNARD: Yes . . . oh, there was a message for you in the Communications Room – er, the VAT man. Your '69 returns. *(Jim looks puzzled.)* VAT 69.

JIM: Oh. Ah. Yes. Thanks. *(Exit.)*

(Bernard leads Humphrey out of earshot of the Arabs.)

HUMPHREY: I'm rapidly coming to the conclusion, Bernard, that the Minister has had almost as many urgent messages as he can take.

BERNARD: Well, I've just found out the most terrible thing, Sir Humphrey.

HUMPHREY: Dear me.

BERNARD: This contract was obtained by bribery.

HUMPHREY: Of course. All contracts in Kumran are obtained by bribery. Everybody knows that. It's perfectly all right as long as nobody knows.

BERNARD: But shouldn't we tell the Minister?

HUMPHREY: Certainly not!

BERNARD: But if everybody knows.

HUMPHREY: Everybody *else*. You do not let a minister know what everybody else knows, Bernard. *(To approaching Arab.)* Ah, Highness, how very nice to see you.

(Jim appears, now very drunk. He goes up to Humphrey.)

JIM: Ah. Lawrence of Arabia. There's a message for you in the Communications Room.

HUMPHREY: Oh? Who is it?

JIM: Napoleon.

(Cut to Jim's office. Bernard and Humphrey are listening to Jim reading from paper.)

JIM: 'It is alleged in *Le Monde* that the recent British Electronic Systems contract with Kumran was won by bribery.' Do you hear this, Humphrey?

HUMPHREY: Yes, indeed, Minister.

JIM: 'It is said that this is part of a hideous web of corruption woven by Western industrial countries and Third World governments that forms a blot on our modern civilization.'

BERNARD: Webs don't form blots, Minister.

JIM: What?

BERNARD: Well, spiders don't have any ink, you see, only cuttlefish.

JIM *(perplexed)*: Spiders don't have cuttlefish . . . what are you *talking* about?

BERNARD: No, I know, you see . . .

HUMPHREY: Thank you, Bernard.

JIM: Isn't this terrible, printing baseless accusations like this?

HUMPHREY: Oh, yes, yes. Terrible.

JIM: Baksheesh . . . palm-greasing . . . good God, we're British.

HUMPHREY: Absolutely, Minister.

JIM: And yet it's not like the F.T. to print a story like this unless there's *something* behind it. . . . *Is* there something behind it, Humphrey?

BERNARD *(indicating the newspaper)*: I think the sports news is behind it, Minister.

JIM: I want to know the truth, Humphrey.

HUMPHREY: I don't think you do, Minister.

JIM: Will you answer a direct question?

HUMPHREY: I strongly advise you not to *ask* a direct question.

JIM: Why?

HUMPHREY: It might provoke a direct answer.

JIM: It never has yet. Bernard, what do you know about all

this? Tell me, on your word of honour.

BERNARD: Well, I, er, that is, there was, er, someone did . . .

HUMPHREY: There was a lot of gossip, that's all, Minister. Rumour. Hearsay.

JIM: Bernard?

BERNARD: Well, one of the Kumranis did tell me that he had received . . . er . . .

HUMPHREY: Hearsay, Minister.

JIM: Hearsay?

HUMPHREY: Yes. Bernard heard him say it.

JIM: Are you telling me, Humphrey, that the B.E.S. contract was won by bribery?

HUMPHREY: Oh, Minister, I do wish you wouldn't use words like 'bribery'.

JIM: What would you like me to say? Slush funds – sweeteners – brown envelopes?

HUMPHREY: Minister, these are extremely crude and unworthy expressions for what is no more than creative negotiation. It is the general practice.

JIM: You do realize what you're saying, don't you, Humphrey? I ratified that contract, didn't I? In good faith.

HUMPHREY: Yes indeed Minister.

JIM: And in that communiqué that I issued to the Press I announced a British success, won in a fair fight.

HUMPHREY: Yes, I did wonder about that bit.

JIM: And now you're telling me that it was got by bribery?

HUMPHREY: No, Minister.

JIM: Oh. It was *not* got by bribery?

HUMPHREY: That is not what I said.

JIM: What did you say?

HUMPHREY: I said I am not telling you it was got by bribery.

JIM: Then how would you describe these . . . payments?

HUMPHREY: How does the contract describe them, you mean?

JIM: Yes.

HUMPHREY: Oh well, that's really quite simple – retainers, personal donations, special discounts, miscellaneous outgoings, agents fees, political contributions, management expenses . . .

JIM: And how are these payments made?

HUMPHREY: Well, anything from a numbered account in a Swiss Bank to a fistful of used oncers slipped under the door of the Gents.

JIM: Do you realize how shocking this is?

HUMPHREY: Minister, that is a narrow and parochial view. In other parts of the world they see things quite differently.

JIM: Sin is not a branch of geography, Humphrey.

HUMPHREY: Oh, but it is, Minister. In developing countries the size of the, ah, extra-contractual payment is the means of showing how serious you are about the deal. It's like a publisher's advance to an author – the one who pays the biggest advance is the one who expects the biggest sales, that's all.

(Phone rings. Bernard answers.)

JIM: I just don't believe this – are you saying that winking at corruption is Government policy?

HUMPHREY: Oh *no*, Minister – it could never be Government policy, that is unthinkable. Only Government practice.

BERNARD *(puts phone down)*: That was the Press Office, Minister. It looks as if the papers may want a statement about the Kumran bribery allegation.

JIM: Statement? Well, what am I going to say?

HUMPHREY: I'm sure the Press Office can devise something convincing and meaningless. After all, that's what they're paid for.

JIM: You're a cynic, Humphrey.

HUMPHREY: Cynic. A cynic is what an idealist calls a realist.

JIM: I shall tell the truth. After all, I know nothing of this. Why should I back something that I never approved?

HUMPHREY: But this contract means thousands of British jobs. Millions of export dollars. Surely you're not going to throw all that away because of some small technical irregularity?

JIM: It's not a small technical irregularity. It is corruption.

HUMPHREY: No, Minister – merely a few uncontracted pre-payments.

JIM: Humphrey, I don't expect you to understand this, but Government is not just a matter of fixing and manipulating – there is a *moral* dimension.

HUMPHREY: Oh yes, of course, Minister, the moral dimension. I assure you it is never out of my thoughts.

JIM: So, if this comes up in Parliament, or if questions are asked in the Press, I shall announce an inquiry.

HUMPHREY: Oh, a splendid idea, Minister. I shall be most happy to conduct it.

JIM: No, no, no . . . not an internal inquiry. A *real* inquiry.

HUMPHREY *(alarmed)*: Minister! You can't be serious!

JIM: A real inquiry.

HUMPHREY: No, Minister, I beg you . . .

JIM: Humphrey – the *moral* dimension.

(Cut to the hall of Jim's London flat. The doorbell rings. Annie opens the door; Bernard enters.)

BERNARD: Good evening Mrs. Hacker.

ANNIE: Ah, Bernard, come in. Jim's just coming.

BERNARD: Thank you very much.

JIM *(off)*: That you Bernard?

BERNARD: Yes, Minister.

JIM: Won't be a moment.

BERNARD *(noticing the rosewater jar on display)*: Oh, there's that jar from Kumran.

ANNIE: Yes. Funnily enough, a friend of mine was round here this afternoon and was frightfully interested in it.

BERNARD: Oh, really?

ANNIE: Yes. Her name's Jenny Goodwin – from the *Guardian*.

BERNARD: The *Guardian*?

ANNIE: She asked where it came from.

BERNARD *(hushed)*: A journalist?

ANNIE: Yes. Well, the *Guardian*, anyway. She asked what it was worth. I said about fifty pounds.

BERNARD: You said about fifty pounds.

ANNIE: Yes. Funnily enough, *she* thought it was genuine.

BERNARD: She thought it was genuine.

ANNIE: Yes. Bernard, you sound like an answering machine.

BERNARD: Oh, I'm sorry.

ANNIE: She asked if I'd mind if she rang up the Kumrani Embassy, to ask what it was worth.

BERNARD: To ask what it was worth. *(Pulls himself together.)* So what did you say?

ANNIE: I said, by all means. It *is* only a copy, isn't it, Bernard?

BERNARD *(staring at her)*: Well – so far as I'm . . . er, so I'm led to . . . good gracious is that the time?

(Cut to Jim's office. Humphrey enters. Bernard is arranging

papers on the desk.)

HUMPHREY: Ah, Bernard.

BERNARD: Oh, sorry, Sir Humphrey. The Minister's going to be a few minutes late.

HUMPHREY: Ah, I'll come back. *(Makes to go.)*

BERNARD: Well, actually, Sir Humphrey, I wonder if I could have a word with you?

HUMPHREY: Yes. *(Pause.)* I said yes.

BERNARD: Yes, I know. You see, er . . . *(Anguished pause.)*

HUMPHREY: Something the matter, Bernard? *(More anguished silence.)* Come on – out with it. Did you send the Minister to the wrong dinner? Give him the wrong speech? Show him some papers we didn't mean him to see? *(Bernard shakes his head miserably.)* Worse? *(Bernard nods.)* Much worse? *(Bernard nods again.)* You'd better sit down. *(They sit.)* Tell me about it.

BERNARD: Well, you know that jar the Minister was given in Kumran? Well, the Minister's wife liked it.

HUMPHREY: I expect she did.

BERNARD: And then when I explained the rules to her she looked . . . terribly sad.

HUMPHREY: They always do.

BERNARD: And then she asked was it really worth more than fifty pounds, and she said wouldn't it be marvellous if it wasn't, and she sort of . . . looked at me.

HUMPHREY: But my dear Bernard, a seventeenth-century vase . . .

BERNARD: Yes, I know, I know. But there was this terribly nice Kumrani business man. And we had a . . . a . . . a conversation . . . and he valued it as a copy, not as an original. *(Produces a piece of paper.)* £49·95.

HUMPHREY: And you believed him.

BERNARD: Well, yes, he said he was an expert – and he spoke Arabic awfully well . . . and so I accepted his valuation in good faith. After all, Islam is a jolly good faith.

HUMPHREY: Bernard, you took a grave personal risk. You're lucky nobody has asked any questions.

BERNARD: But that's just it, you see – a journalist from the *Guardian* saw it in the Minister's house and started to ask a lot of questions, and of course Mrs. Hacker said it was a copy, but . . . well, the Press are so horribly suspicious about things.

HUMPHREY: Despicable.

BERNARD: What shall I do?

HUMPHREY: The Minister must be told.

(Jim enters.)

JIM: Morning, Humphrey.

HUMPHREY: Good morning, Minister.

JIM: I'm sorry to keep you.

HUMPHREY: That's all right. You read my submission, Minister?

JIM: Yes I did, and it won't do. I am not going to be accused of sweeping bribery under the carpet. So if questions *are* asked I am going to announce a full independant enquiry chaired by a Q.C.

HUMPHREY: But Minister, you can't. That contract is worth 340 million pounds.

JIM: Get thee behind me, Humphrey. The *moral* dimension.

HUMPHREY: Well, Minister, if there *is* an enquiry, other things may come out too.

JIM: Such as?

HUMPHREY: I'm afraid Bernard has something to tell you.

(Pause. Humphrey and Jim look at Bernard.)

JIM: Well?

BERNARD: Well, you know that jar the Kumranis gave you?

JIM: Yes. It's at the flat now. Most attractive.

BERNARD: Well, I told Mrs. Hacker she could keep it, because I had it valued for less than £50, but I'm not sure, the man who valued it was awfully nice . . . and I told him Mrs. Hacker liked it a lot . . . but he may have been, just, well, being helpful.

JIM: That's all right, Bernard. No-one will ever know. Jolly enterprising of you.

BERNARD: No – Mrs. Hacker told me a journalist had seen it and was asking questions.

JIM *(horrified)*: A journalist?

HUMPHREY: May I just see that valuation? *(Bernard hands it over.)* Hm. The Treasury isn't too happy about valuations written on the backs of menus.

BERNARD: It is a very good menu.

(The phone rings. Bernard answers it.)

JIM: What is it worth, really?

HUMPHREY: Well if it's a copy, what the valuation says, probably.

JIM: And if it's genuine?

HUMPHREY: About five thousand pounds.

JIM: Oh my God – and I kept it!

BERNARD: All right, send him in. *(Puts phone down.)* Minister, Bill Pritchard from the Press Office is coming in to talk to you.

JIM: Not now, Bernard, not now – I'm trying to deal with this terrible problem you've landed me with.

BERNARD: That's what he wants to talk to you about. *(Bill Pritchard is ushered in.)*

JIM: Well?

BILL: Minister, the Foreign and Commonwealth Office are in a frightful state. It seems that Mrs. Hacker has told the *Guardian* that that extremely valuable seventeenth-century thing presented to you by the Kumrani Government was a copy. The *Guardian* phoned the Kumrani Embassy for their comments, and now the Kumran Government are incensed at the suggestion that they insulted Britain by giving you a worthless gift. The F.C.O. say it's building up into the biggest diplomatic incident since 'Death of a Princess'. *(Jim tries to speak, and fails.)* And there is a reporter outside from the *Guardian* demanding to see you right away. *(Jim's mouth is still too dry to utter a sound.)*

BERNARD: Um . . . *(They all look at him.)*

JIM: Yes, Bernard?

BERNARD: Minister . . . what . . . what are you . . .

JIM: Bernard, my duty is clear. I have no choice.

BERNARD: No choice?

JIM: No choice, Bernard. I didn't ask you to lie to my wife about the value of that gift, did I?

BERNARD: No, but . . .

JIM: Bernard, I realize you acted from the purest possible motives; but I'm sorry – there can be no excuse for falsifying a document.

BERNARD: But I . . .

JIM: Let me continue, please. I cannot have it said that I asked you to do this – no more, Humphrey, than I can have it said that I connived at bribery and corruption in our business dealings. Enough is enough. So I'm afraid if this journalist asks me straight questions on either of these subjects I shall have to give her straight answers. The moral dimension.

HUMPHREY: Yes, Minister, I agree with you. I see now that there is a moral dimension to everything. Will you tell the Press about the Communications Room, or shall I? You know – all that Scotch in Kumran.

(Jim is appalled. Bernard brightens up considerably.)

JIM: You mean to tell me that if I say . . . *(He points at Bernard.)* . . . then you will tell . . . *(He points at Humphrey.)* . . . and drop me in . . .

HUMPHREY: In the moral dimension.

JIM: But this is completely different – it's not the same thing at all.

HUMPHREY: Why?

JIM: Drinking? It's not corruption.

HUMPHREY: No – it's just deceit, that's all.

JIM: Deceit?

HUMPHREY: We have deceived the Kumranis. I am wracked with guilt, tormented by the knowledge that we have violated their solemn and sacred Islamic Law in their own country. Sooner or later we'll have to own up and admit that it was all your idea.

JIM: It wasn't!

BERNARD
HUMPHREY }: It was.

JIM: It wasn't . . . was it?

HUMPHREY *(to Bernard)*: Is it 50 lashes or 100?

BILL: Minister, I must ask you meet this journalist, or she'll write something terrible anyway.

JIM: Yes, yes, all right, yes . . . *(Exit Bill.)* What am I going to say?

HUMPHREY: Well, may I suggest that attack is the best form of defence?

JIM: Attack . . . attack, yes, good thinking, Humphrey. Yes, got it.

(Bill re-enters, followed by a young woman.)

BILL: Minister, may I introduce Miss Jenny Goodwin from the *Guardian*.

JIM *(charming)*: Ah, do come in, sit down, won't you, Jenny. I may call you Jenny, may I not?

JENNY: If you like.

JIM: Now – what seems to be the trouble?

JENNY: Two things, really, Minister. Both of them rather worrying to the public. The first is a story that you may have seen in the French Press – it's about corruption in B.E.S. getting the Kumrani contract.

JIM: Complete nonsense.

JENNY: But they quoted reports of payments to officials.

JIM: Really, this is absolutely typical. A British company slogs its guts out to win orders, create jobs, earn dollars – and what does it get from the media? A smear campaign.

JENNY: But if they won by bribery . . .

JIM: There is no question of bribery. I've had a full internal enquiry, and all these so-called payments have been identified.

JENNY: What as?

JIM: As, er . . .

HUMPHREY: Commission fees. Administrative overheads.

JIM: Operating costs. Managerial surcharges.

BERNARD: Introduction expenses. Miscellaneous outgoings.

JIM: We have looked into every brown envelope . . . er, every account book, and everything is completely in order.

JENNY: I see.

JIM: And may I say one further thing. Allegations of this nature are symptomatic of a very sick society, for which I am afraid the media must take its share of the blame.

JENNY: The media?

JIM: Why are you putting thousands of British jobs at risk? I am calling on the Press Council to censure the Press for its appalling lack of professional standards in running this story. The Council, and indeed the House of Commons, must be concerned about the standards which have applied in this disgraceful matter: and pressure will be brought to bear to make sure that this sort of gutter press reporting is not repeated.

JENNY *(discomfited)*: I see. Well, there is this other question. It's about the rosewater jar apparently presented to you in Kumran.

JIM: Yes?

JENNY: Well, I saw it in your flat, actually.

JIM: Well yes, we're keeping it there, temporarily.

JENNY: Temporarily?

JIM: Oh yes. It's very valuable, you know.

JENNY: Mrs. Hacker said that it was an imitation.

JIM: Burglars, girl, burglars! We didn't want gossip going around, until we could get rid of it.

JENNY: Get rid of it.

JIM: Yes, I'm presenting it to our local museum, as soon as I get up to the constituency at the weekend. Well, I can't hold on to it, you know. It's Government property. Now . . . what was your question?

JENNY: No, er . . . that's all right, actually . . . I, er . . . no, no, no . . . that's fine.

JIM: Nothing more?

JENNY: No, no, that's all.

JIM *(ushering her out)*: Well, good of you to drop in.

JENNY: Thank you, Minister.

JIM: Goodbye, Jenny.

(Exit Jenny.)

HUMPHREY: Superb, Minister.

BERNARD: Thank you, Minister.

JIM: Well, it was nothing. One must stick by one's friends, eh, Humphrey? Eh, Bernard? Loyalty!

(He stands behind them and places a hand on each of their shoulders.)

HUMPHREY }
BERNARD } *(uncomfortably)*: Yes, Minister.